# MY EARLY LIFE

To our friend Professor Miller,

*The Myth of Arab Piracy in the Gulf*

*The British Occupation of Aden*

*The Fragmentation of the Omani Empire*

# MY EARLY LIFE

Sultan bin Muhammad al-Qasimi

*Translated from the Arabic by Dr Domenyk Eades*

Edited by Dr Ahmed Ali,
Brian Pridham and Dr Khaled Hroub

BLOOMSBURY

LONDON · BERLIN · NEW YORK · SYDNEY

First published in Great Britain 2011

First published in 2009 in Arabic as *Sard Al That* by Al Qasimi Publications

Copyright © 2011 by Sultan bin Muhammad al-Qasimi

The moral right of the author has been asserted

No part of this book may be used or reproduced in any manner
whatsoever without written permission from the Publisher except in the
case of brief quotations embodied in critical articles or reviews

All images reproduced in this book are from the author's private collection

Bloomsbury Publishing Plc
36 Soho Square
London W1D 3QY

www.bloomsbury.com

Bloomsbury Publishing, London, New York and Berlin
A CIP catalogue record for this book is available from the British Library

ISBN 978 1 4088 1420 8

10 9 8 7 6 5 4 3 2 1

Typeset by Hewer Text UK Ltd, Edinburgh
Printed in Dubai by Oriental Press

# Contents

# PARTIAL FAMILY TREE OF AL-QASIMI SHAIKHS

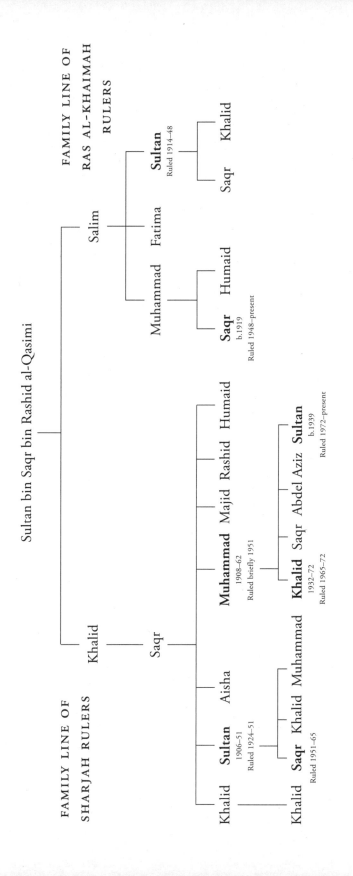

Sultan bin Saqr bin Rashid al-Qasimi

FAMILY LINE OF SHARJAH RULERS

FAMILY LINE OF RAS AL-KHAIMAH RULERS

Khalid

Salim

Saqr

Muhammad   Fatima

Aisha

Sultan
1906–51
Ruled 1924–51

Khalid

**Muhammad**
1908–62
Ruled briefly 1951

Majid   Rashid   Humaid

**Saqr**
b.1919
Ruled 1948–present

Humaid

**Sultan**
Ruled 1914–48

Saqr   Khalid

Khalid

**Saqr** Khalid Muhammad
Ruled 1951–65

**Khalid**
1932–72
Ruled 1965–72

Saqr   Abdel Aziz

**Sultan**
b.1939
Ruled 1972–present

# *Foreword*

THIS BOOK IS A DOCUMENT of the history of my family and my country over a period of twenty-nine years. While I have omitted much that was irrelevant, I have also chosen not to include many events that involved people who have passed away and whose stories might upset memories that are better kept within the folds of forgetfulness.

Many individuals supported me while I was writing this book. My wife and children listened to my recollection of the events that I had witnessed throughout my early life and persistently encouraged me to write the book as a permanent record for others to read, now and in the future. Several of my close associates assisted me in collecting, from different sources, copies of some of the supporting archival documents relevant to the events mentioned in the book. Finally, the translators, editors and many others in the publishing industry have worked very hard to produce this excellent English edition of the book. The perseverance and dedication of all involved are greatly appreciated.

May Allah forgive us all.

Sultan bin Muhammad al-Qasimi,
September 2010

I

*Childhood Days*

I WAS BORN ON SUNDAY, 14 Jumada al-Ula 1358, corresponding to 2 July 1939, and became aware of what was happening
in the world around me even before my fifth birthday. In the
spring of 1944 the Second World War was still raging; British
troops and warplanes were already in the British base attached
to the airfield in Sharjah and the United States had decided
to send its forces to Lydda in Palestine, Habbaniya in Iraq,
Bahrain and Sharjah for training, before later deploying them
to North Africa.

A team of American military engineers arrived in Sharjah at
the beginning of 1944 and built a training camp for the American
army to the east of the British base there; the American troops
themselves arrived in early May. My father, in his capacity as
Deputy to his brother, the Ruler of Sharjah, then in India, paid
a courtesy visit to General Lucius Clay, Commanding Officer
of the troops (I met him in New York in 1974, when he was
Chief Executive of Lehman Brothers), who invited us aboard an
amphibious open-top vehicle known as the DUKW, or, more

familiarly, as 'Duck'. I sat between the Commanding Officer and my father, while my older brother Khalid, his friend 'Umran bin Taryam and an American soldier sat in the back. The vehicle drove through the town of Sharjah and then took to the Creek, becoming a boat; it then left the Creek and crossed the dry land of Al-Shush (a sandy spit dividing the Creek from the open sea), the boat becoming a vehicle again, before entering the rough sea. Now it was once more a boat, rising and falling as it struggled against the waves, and we were in the open sea; I became seasick and vomited over the Commanding Officer's uniform. In annoyance, the officer turned the wheel towards Sharjah, bringing our boat trip to an end.

On 8 September 1944, a military plane ditched in the sea just off the village of Layyah in Sharjah. This aircraft, a Consolidated Liberator II bomber, number AL 550, belonged to the British Royal Air Force and was trying unsuccessfully to gain height after taking off from Sharjah airport. All the crew members, who were the only people aboard, were rescued. I went to the shore with my brother Khalid and found some coloured pens thrown up on the shore by the waves near the spot where the aircraft had come down. My brother set about collecting the pens and giving them to me.

## Our house

We lived in a house adjoining the house of my uncle, Shaikh Sultan bin Saqr al-Qasimi; it belonged to his wife, Latifa bint Sa'id. Between the two houses there was a fence of date-palm leaves and a gate shared by both houses. I cannot remember my uncle and his family being in that house, nor do I remember the death of his two daughters, 'Azza and 'Aliya, there. But I do remember the opening that I and my uncle's two sons, 'Abdullah, who was older than me, and Su'ud, who was younger, made in the palm-leaf fence when we wanted to pass from one house to the other. I used to watch the opening with a touch of fear and personal foreboding; I fancied I could see the legs of a *jinni*, like *mihmas* handles (a *mihmas* is a shallow pan with a long handle, used by the Bedouin to roast coffee beans), as he ran from the toilet at the corner of the house to the room of my uncle's daughters in the other corner, in order to kill them. Because of bad memories associated with the death of his daughters my uncle abandoned that house and had a new palm-leaf house built with great haste.

The palm-leaf fence used to divide the deserted house of my uncle from my father's house which was always full of people. My father had a large entourage of family, neighbours, slaves and servants: guests would attend one of my father's *majlises* (a public reception area outside the house) – the large *majlis* for the public and the small one for leading personalities. Not a day passed without a feast in our house: plates piled with food were passed out of the three doors of the house, and others were passed to the outside benches of the general *majlis* where hungry people would flock, this being a period of famine brought on by the Second World War.

The western gate of our house opened onto a courtyard with the houses of my uncles around it, and also Bin Rakkadh's house whose sons, Ibrahim and Ali (who were both working on the British base), used to bring me English magazines which I was too young to read but I enjoyed the pictures. Close by the courtyard was a house whose wall was crumbling; a large store-room protruded from it and its door was always open to the courtyard. This was called Al-Duwaish's house. My uncle Majid kept a madman in there, secured with an iron chain fixed to a rock. Whenever the madman sensed that someone was passing near the storeroom he would rush towards the door, shrieking. Passers-by imagined that he was free, until the chain stopped him from going beyond the storeroom door. The way through the courtyard, passing by the madman's door, led to the mosque or the market, or to the house of the Mutawwaʿ, or teacher, Faris bin ʿAbd al-Rahman, a Najdi from Saudi Arabia who was Imam of the mosque and taught the children at his house. (In some countries the Mutawwaʿ is an enforcer of Islamic proprieties but here the word denotes a preacher and teacher.) The house of the Mutawwaʿ Faris was close to our family houses, but fear that the madman might escape stopped me from going there to school. Then the madman suddenly disappeared, the wall around Al-Duwaish's house was repaired and it was incorporated into my uncle Majid's house. With my mind at rest I was able to go regularly to the Mutawwaʿ's house. I was still young, learning the *juz' ʿamma* – the final one-thirtieth of the Qur'an and traditionally the first step in memorising it – but the older boys and girls were completing the Qur'an, one after the other. Completing the Qur'an did not mean memorising it: it meant being able to read all of it very well and memorising the *juz' ʿamma*.

Those who completed the Qur'an graduated from the school after the Mutawwaʿ or the female Mutawwaʿ had carried out the laudation of God. A boy would be dressed in clean clothes or, sometimes, new clothes, while the sons of the Shaikhs or the rich would put on a gold *khanjar*, or dagger, with headcloth and headband. The boy would graduate together with his contemporaries, led by the Mutawwa' or someone deputising for him, repeating the invocation of God with the boys behind him saying Amen, as one, in a loud voice like a bellow: AMEN. The Mutawwa' or his deputy then went from door to door collecting donations.

The daughters of Shaikhs and the rich would wear gold chains and pendants on their heads and their chests, and their hands would be dyed with henna. The eastern gate of our house opened to the courtyard and the children used to enjoy playing there until late at night.

## My uncle's deserted house

The fence dividing our house from my uncle's abandoned house fell down and couldn't be repaired, so my father ordered it to be removed. Several years later, it was decided to open up a door to the main room in the empty house, facing ours, and to close our main door facing the empty house. My sister Na'ima's nanny, Jumai'a, was housed in the storeroom while the second adjoining room was used as a store for cow and sheep fodder. Indinghi, my father's slave, was responsible for the fodder; he was a tall man of African origin and often used to carry me on his shoulders. Nanny Jumai'a became ill and no treatment was of any use: she died in her storeroom. As for Indinghi, I found him dead one day, on a heap of animal fodder, in the adjoining room.

At that time, my father's armed escort, 'Ayyid bin Khusaif, married a woman called Maryam and began to build her a house made of date-palm leaves in the courtyard fronting the eastern gate of our house. He fixed the wall of his house to the wall of the abandoned house of my uncle Shaikh Sultan bin Saqr al-Qasimi, in the area of the toilet where the *jinni* lived, as we children imagined. Suddenly, this quiet woman, from whom we had never heard a sound since she came to live in that house, changed into something very akin to a devil – her hair uncovered and dishevelled, wild-eyed, her screaming ringing out, and foaming at the mouth. Men were called. Two of them held her hands and pinned them down as if she was being crucified, while another whipped her back with some force, shouting to the *jinni*, 'Be gone . . . Be gone . . . Be gone!'

Maryam's eyes were staring, and when her gaze met mine I trembled for fear that the *jinni* would leave her eyes and leap into mine. But her eyelids closed and her head soon fell on to her chest as the man with the whip continued beating and shouting 'Be gone . . . Be gone . . . Be gone!' until the whip was falling on a lifeless body.

That night, fire broke out in the house although nobody was there; people rushed to put it out and suddenly the sound of shots rang out from the source of the blaze. The firefighters fell back and the fire destroyed the house. 'Ayyid bin Khusaif arrived in a hurry and the people grabbed him accusingly: 'Why did you leave your ammunition in the house?' 'I didn't leave my ammunition in the house,' said 'Ayyid bin Khusaif, 'I've got it on me.' It turned out later that the sound of shots was caused by the explosion of dried lemon pips.

## Sharjah Fort

This fort lay to the south of our house. The buildings were separated only by the wide lane leading to the city's markets, so that our windows overlooked it. Caravans went back and forth laden with items for whoever wanted to buy or sell. Here a man is being escorted by an *askari*, a policeman, with a rifle, who pushes him along whenever he resists, walking towards the fort. Another is returning from it, head bowed and noticeable only by his sobbing. Another man strides along; he has spruced himself up and is deep in thought, embellishing the words he is going to use to the Shaikh. If he comes back wreathed in smiles he has been rewarded generously: but if he comes back muttering incoherently his hopes have been dashed. And we observe all of this, morning and evening.

Sharjah Fort is a square building with four main parts. The first of them is the room which is used as a *majlis* for important people: it lies in the south-eastern corner of the fort. Next is the Mashraf – a square-sectioned tower commanding the south-west of the fort and used by the guards. To the north-west is the Kubs, a round tower, also used by the guards. The Mahlusa is a huge tower, its name derived from its unusual architectural style whose upper parts were used by the guards and whose lower floor was a grim prison. The front of the fort looked out to the square; the fort's huge door was decorated with nail heads – dome-shaped in glittering bronze. Between this door and the Mahlusa, in its afternoon shade, there was a large wooden bench with supports, and at each end some wooden steps leading up to it. There was also a large cannon, called Al-Raqqas, on wooden wheels, and another smaller one, also on wheels.

To the left of the doorway was a custodial jail; it had a window giving onto the square that enabled a prisoner to speak to his relatives and above the window there was a small hole for ventilation. The door to this jail opened onto the inner hall of the main gate, called Al-Isbah and heavily guarded. There was an accused person in this jail who had committed robbery in the past; his right hand had been cut off for his earlier crimes but one night he stole a small bronze cannon. It was difficult for someone with one hand and a weak constitution to lift that cannon and make away with it through the high ventilation opening, but he still managed to escape from the jail. They tracked him and found him in a heap of animal fodder, still hugging the cannon.

After this jail came the provisions store, run by one of the Shaikh's slaves called Ibn Kalban, who distributed kerosene and charcoal, plus some food, to the ruling family's houses. Next along were garages for cars, with a door opening into the stables. Over these areas was the room where the Shaikh held his *majlis*, in front of which was an open terrace followed by a covered arcade. All of it gave onto the front courtyard of the fort so that, in the evening, when Shaikh Sultan's brothers and their children came together to have their supper, people would mass in front of Sharjah Fort, singly or in groups, to listen to news broadcasts about the war (this was in 1945). They could hear the radio from one of the windows in the room on the upper floor of the fort.

Half of the people supported the Allies and half supported the Axis powers. The news from the German radio station, with the sharp tongue of the Iraqi broadcaster Yunus Bahri, would infuriate the supporters of the Allies, just as the news coming from the BBC Middle East Service through the voice of the Syrian Munir Shamma angered the supporters of the Axis. From the windows overlooking the fort's front square we children watched the fighting between the two sides.

Elsewhere in the fort, in the southern part, lived the mother of Shaikh Saqr bin Sultan al-Qasimi; the northern part was the living quarters of Shaikh Saqr, his wife and his children. Facing the fort was a large building, half of it completely finished and the other half more like a shelter: for that reason it was called Al-Sabat (the Arcade). Large numbers of Bedouin would stay there as guests of the Shaikh. To the north of the Arcade was a well for washing and on the south side there was a camel stall. Between the Arcade and the fort a heavy ship's mast was embedded; its upper part was pitch-black. Lawbreakers such as thieves and criminals were tied to the mast and this was known as *hatb al-tauba* (the penitential log). When a thief or criminal was tied to the mast we boys would hang around while he was being flogged. We argued about the black part of the mast. Some of the boys said that the upper part of it would be set alight and the fire would burn downwards in the direction of the thief; when he felt the fire getting close to him he would confess straight away. I said that we were there every day to watch the punishments but we had never seen a fire burning and this black part had been there for as long as we could remember.

I asked my father about the black part of the mast and he told me this story:

'In the time of my father Shaikh Saqr bin Khalid al-Qasimi, Ruler of Sharjah, there was a blind black man known as Basiduh who lived in Al-'Ali quarter of Sharjah. On a stormy day, with the southerly wind called the *suhaili* blowing, Basiduh went out, finding his way with his stick, to the market to beg for some fish from the fishermen. As soon as he got back to his dilapidated tent of palm leaves and canvas, and lit the fire to grill his fish, the tent caught alight and burnt Basiduh to death.

'The fire wasn't content with just Basiduh and his tent but spread through the palm-leaf houses and sent its flames out to the west, dancing through the burning houses. The blaze reached for the clouds, throwing out the lightest fragments after the fire had destroyed and devoured the houses, leaving behind sheep and cattle charred in their stalls. The flying sparks and cinders were swept by the strong winds towards Sharjah Creek, where a pearl fishing boat called Al Ghalib, owned by Ibn Madhkur, was lying close to the shore. A burning splinter carried by the wind lodged in the top of the boat's mast and the fire began to eat away at the mast from the top downwards, until it reached a height of a fathom or so above the deck of the boat. Shaikh Saqr bin Khalid al-Qasimi, the Ruler of Sharjah, was seen riding along the shore on his horse and he ordered the cable that held the mast in the boat to be cut and the remains of the mast to be thrown in the sea to extinguish the fire. He then ordered it to be moved to the front of the fort and embedded in the earth so that thieves and criminals could be tied to it. It then became known as *hatb al-tauba*.'

Not long ago that section of the boat's mast was used for tying up divers who feigned illness to avoid going down to the seabed to harvest pearls, out of fear of the sharks that used to attack them, or because of shortness of breath. Sometimes divers would be pulled up raving about the *jinnis* they imagined they had seen on the sea floor. Some had their eardrums affected by the great pressure of the water on them; they were treated by being branded beneath the ears. Later on, that same log was used to tie up accused people who were to be flogged in order to extract their confessions.

To the south of the *hatb al-tauba* is a collection of old guns, their barrels supported near their muzzles on palm trunks, that were never used at all. The cannon that was used for firing a salute for a guest or to proclaim the Eid, the religious feast after the holy month of Ramadan or after practising pilgrimage to Macca (otherwise known as Hajj), was the small one on wooden wheels. It happened that Amir Su'ud bin 'Abd al-'Aziz Al Su'ud from Saudi Arabia was a guest of Sharjah en route to India, when he was passing through Sharjah airport. Shaikh Sultan bin Saqr al-Qasimi, the Ruler of Sharjah, invited him to take coffee in the *majlis* of the fort, and orders were given to the guard who was assigned to the cannon to fire one shot as the guest stepped out of the car at the door of the fort. This guard, together with a group of other guards, tried to push the small cannon from its place near the door where the guest would arrive, to some distance away. But they were unable to move it, and it stayed stubbornly in place.

The guards called for us to help them – we were a group of boys who had gathered to watch the guest arriving at the fort. Standing close by us were two men who were attendants of Shaikh Muhammad bin Hamad al-Shamsi, brother of Shaikh Rashid bin Hamad al-Shamsi, the Shaikh of Hamasa. Shaikh Muhammad was staying along with his companions as guests of

my father in the private *majlis* of our house; one was called Hass
and the other Jumai'.

They joined us in pushing the gun but it refused to move, so
the guard decided to use one of the old cannons, propped up
on palm trunks. He began stuffing gunpowder and rags into
the gun as we clustered around him and the rust was flaking off
its surface and piling up on the ground. After he had finished
loading the cannon he put some of the gunpowder in the narrow
aperture at the back of the barrel. When the guest arrived he put
a burning ember to the tip of a palm-leaf rib and asked us to
stand back. As soon as he touched the flame to the back of the
gun it exploded. Fragments shot out in a cloud of smoke and
Jumai' fell to the ground: he had been struck by a shard that tore
the flesh from his cheek and exposed his teeth.

The British used to bring a film projector once a week to
the camel station to show their victories – but not their defeats
– in the Second World War. That place was full of ticks and
camel ticks, bigger than the rest, that fell from the camels; in
the course of the film the audience used to scratch their legs and
feet because of the bites of the ticks that were sucking the blood
from their bodies.

The doorway to the stables abutting the fort on its southern
side, whose western wall was the remains of Sharjah town wall,
gave on to the enclosure of the mosque for the Bedouin. I used
to practise horse-riding in the stable yard, and when the time
came for my cousins, who were older than me, to go out into
the desert on their horses I asked Sa'id al-Khail (Sa'id of the
horses), who was responsible for teaching us horse-riding, if I
could go out with them and he agreed. But he was afraid of the

horse bolting with me so he decided to take all of us on a tour of the roads of Sharjah town, including the *suq*, the market. So we came to the western fish *suq* and there was a row of women with different vegetables spread out on the ground: radishes, onions, tomatoes, melons and sweet basil.

My horse got close to the women, who left their vegetables and ran, and it began to devour the vegetables and to trample the melons and watermelons. I couldn't control the animal and Sa'id al-Khail rushed up on his horse to push mine into the centre of the group of horses. But then his horse started to trample over what remained of the vegetables. People in the *suq* started shouting and waving their arms so that the horses broke away and rushed through the *suq*. Thank God no one was harmed, but the people complained to Shaikh Sultan bin Saqr al-Qasimi, who reprimanded all of us, compensated those who had suffered any loss and issued an order banning horses from entering the *suqs*, markets and streets of Sharjah.

# 2

*Shaikh Sultan bin Saqr al-Qasimi*

S HAIKH SULTAN BIN SAQR AL-QASIMI had been Ruler of Sharjah since 1924, and his brother, Shaikh Muhammad bin Saqr al-Qasimi, was Deputy Ruler. Their brother, Shaikh Majid bin Saqr al-Qasimi, would sit in the 'Arsa charcoal suq listening to people's complaints, for him to settle or to pass on to the town's qadi, Islamic judge, who applied the Shar' (Islamic law) in order to fairly and justly resolve disputes among the people. The qadi at that time was Shaikh Saif bin Muhammad bin Mijlad, to whom people brought their suits in his crowded majlis. He would send his judgements to Shaikh Sultan bin Saqr al-Qasimi for them to be implemented or approved. The Shaikh's wazir (Minister) was Sayyid Ibrahim bin Muhammad al-Midfa': his work was confined to the exchange of messages and official relations with outside bodies.

## Feast days

People would be looking out for the crescent moon denoting Eid at sunset, after the evening prayer. In that complete silence the sound of the cannon roared out, announcing that the next day was Eid. After that you could hear the buzzing of the people crowding the *suqs* – people who had been late in preparing themselves for the Eid, or who came just to watch. One might have come to buy clothes for the Eid; the next waiting his turn with the 'beautifier', i.e. the barber; another one might have come to buy what was needed for *fuwala*, for offering to guests. *Fuwala* was comprised of sweets such as *manfush*, and *bashmak*, made from crushed sesame seed tahina paste; it was also called *herda*. Opposite the shop of Taimur the confectioner (it was he who made and sold the sweets) was a shop with a mill; a blindfolded donkey would turn it incessantly and was known as the *herda* donkey. It gave rise to a saying: if you said to someone, 'Don't load that worker too much,' he would say, 'Don't worry, he's the *herda* donkey.'

On the morning of the Eid people came out in their finery and went to the prayer ground a kilometre and a half from the city. There was a concrete pulpit there with three steps, on which the preacher stood, facing the crowded rows. The preacher for Eid and Fridays was Shaikh Saif bin Muhammad bin Mijlad, who had a loud voice. The men and boys were in the front rows and at the head of them were Shaikh Sultan bin Saqr al-Qasimi, his brothers and other relatives and the town dignitaries. The women were in the back rows and there were few of them. When the Eid prayer was finished they all went towards the town, and as soon as one of the guards in the fort saw the people coming in their white clothes he gave the order to fire the gun. Whoever heard the sound of the gun knew for certain and could say 'Eid is here'.

People flocked to the fort to congratulate Shaikh Sultan bin Saqr al-Qasimi on the Eid. Among the crowd would be a group of guards employed by the Shaikh for guarding the British air-base; they were of Omani origin and lived near the airport in a place known as Al-Manakh. Their head was called Nasir al-Zaidi. When they got to the fort square they would start singing and dancing; prominent among them were two men who had swords and shields in their hands and would act out a duel. At the end of the scene one of them stabbed the other and slaughtered him, stretching him out on the ground; finally, he prodded the victim with his sword, who then got back onto his feet. The children would be hanging around watching the play-acting and as soon as it finished ran through the lanes and from house to house asking for Eid gifts – a small amount of money given to children on that day.

In the evening of the same day, men, boys, girls and infants flocked to the Rolla (banyan) tree that casts a wide shadow. They would hang ropes on the larger branches of the Rolla tree and the girls would sit in two rows on the ropes; each girl would twist her fingers and feet in the rope on which the girl opposite her was sitting and a swing would be made by eight girls. The boys pushed it for them with great care. Sweets and almonds were on sale beneath the tree. The Shaikh of Sharjah sat on a big chair, surrounded by his relatives and the dignitaries of the town, receiving the Eid congratulations; the 'iyala dance, a war dance, was performed near them.

On Fridays, Shaikh Sultan used to leave one of his houses or the fort, heading towards the Friday mosque, followed by his retinue which was led by a guard carrying a rifle to defend the Shaikh. The Shaikh himself would carry a gold curved sword known as the *kattarah*.

## The Falaj farm

My uncle Shaikh Sultan bin Saqr al-Qasimi set up a large farm in the Falaj area to the east of Burj Khuzam and built a rest-house near it. The farm comprised two wells connected to two water pumps that fed two large reservoirs. The western reservoir was reserved for bathing and was covered with a palm-leaf pergola on which jasmine bushes climbed; their flowers would fall onto the heads of the bathers. The jasmine bushes were grown in a strong container in the middle of the pool covered in glazed tiles decorated with different roses. Around the reservoir were aromatic plants, and herds of gazelle ran here and there.

My uncle Shaikh Sultan used to take his brothers and all the sons of the family with him to the farm. His brothers would ride with him in his private car while the sons rode in a big vehicle like a lorry, singing as they went.

## Shaikh Sultan mediates in the Ras al-Khaimah affair

Early one morning in the first week of February 1948, when I was nine years old, I was sitting with my younger sister Na'ima on a hill overlooking the road between the palm groves and Ras al-Khaimah, one of the golden-coloured hills of Kharran; we were building houses of sand moistened by the rain that had fallen at dawn that day. We decorated the houses with the wild flowers we gathered, bright and multicoloured.

The whole area was cloaked in silence. The morning breeze brushed our faces with breaths of cool wind; if we looked to the east our gaze fell on the plains studded with *samr* trees (*Acacia tortilis*) that extended as far as the foothills of the tall mountains stretching to the north, before meeting with a knot of green on the western edges of the plains. This green knot represented a collection of small villages interleaved with tall palm trees. If we turned our gaze to the north we could see the Ras al-Khaimah creek and, on its banks, the city of Ras al-Khaimah to the west; the village of Mu'airidh to the east; and the creek's lagoon stretching to the south towards the sand dunes of Kharran. These were separated from the hills by an area of *sabkha*, or salt flats, covered by tamarisk bushes and some *ghaf* trees (*Prosopis cineraria*) near the sand dunes, where the cattle sometimes came to drink from a shallow pit in which rainwater would collect.

To the south of us was a fort made of mud called the fort of Shaikh Sultan bin Salim al-Qasimi; we could see poking out from its battlements two rifles pointing towards someone coming from Ras al-Khaimah. Suddenly, from the battlement a voice shouted, 'Stop . . . stop,' and the person coming from Ras al-Khaimah together with four women fell to the ground as they were climbing the hill on which we were sitting. The man shouted out, sobbing (and terrifying with his hoarse voice and frightening appearance): 'We flee from death and now we face death again.' A voice replied from the fort: 'Sukoun . . . Sukoun [that was his name], you are safe here.' Sukoun replied, 'O Saqr! O Khalid!'

Sukoun was in the service of Shaikha 'Aisha bint Saqr al-Qasimi, the mother of Saqr and Khalid, the two teenage sons of Shaikh Sultan bin Salim al-Qasimi, Ruler of Ras al-Khaimah. The women, who went to our house, told us about a revolution in Ras al-Khaimah led by Shaikh Saqr bin Muhammad al-Qasimi, the paternal nephew of Shaikh Sultan bin Salim al-Qasimi, and that both Saqr and Khalid had fled Ras al-Khaimah, but there was no news of them.

I was waiting outside the house for a car that I could hear coming towards us; it turned out to be our own car and my father got out – he had gone out in the morning in the car, driven by 'Abdallah Banderi. Two youths got out with him; they were Saqr and Khalid, the two sons of his sister Shaikha 'Aisha bint Saqr al-Qasimi, wife of Shaikh Sultan bin Salim al-Qasimi, Ruler of Ras al-Khaimah. My father's guard 'Ayyid bin Khusaif was with them; they went into the outside *majlis*, a tent a short way from a collection of tents that made up the living quarters, and my father took me with him into the house. He recounted what had happened:

'When I heard the news that Shaikh Saqr bin Muhammad bin Salim al-Qasimi [the mother of  Shaikh Saqr bin Muhammad bin Salim al-Qasimi was Hassa bint Saqr al-Qasimi, half-sister of my father Muhammad bin Saqr al-Qasimi, not his full sister] had occupied Ras al-Khaimah fort, and that Saqr and Khalid were there in Ras al-Khaimah, I hurried to rescue them.'

Father said that he had gone to the house of Shaikh Humaid bin Muhammad al-Qasimi and found that Khalid bin Sultan had taken refuge there. When he had asked about Saqr he was told that Saqr had fled on a motorcycle from his house in Ras al-Khaimah early in the morning. I said that I had seen a motorcycle early that same morning speeding along the road below the hill, coming from the town of Ras al-Khaimah towards the east. My father said, 'That's right. Saqr had fled to some of his friends in the village of Khatt; I found out his whereabouts after enquiring into the route of the motorcycle mentioned by Sultan, and now they're with me in the *majlis*.'

The news that Saqr and Khalid were in the *majlis* spread through the house and immediately it was filled with ululations from the women followers of Shaikha 'Aisha, the mother of the boys. The women fought to get to the *majlis* to kiss the hands of Saqr and Khalid. My father said that he would take them to their mother, his sister, in Sharjah and I said, 'I'll go with you.' Father simply said to my mother, 'Bring him some clothes.' It was about midday when we got in the car to go to Sharjah, after having had lunch. I sat with my father in the front seat and in the back were Saqr and Khalid, the two sons of Shaikh Sultan bin Salim al-Qasimi, with my father's military escort, 'Ayyid bin Khusaif. An Omani guest of my father also rode with them; he was from the Ja'lan, in the south-east of Oman, and was a mild-tempered man – good-hearted, a joker, laughing and funny; he had a white beard and a dark complexion. He wore a silver *khanjar*, and was dressed in a white gown and a woollen head cloth.

My father and his sister's two sons were despondent after their calamity and the car was making groaning noises as if it too had been wounded, leaning to right and left as it followed the sand track. The Ja'lani leant forward into the gap between the front seats where I was sitting with my father and the rear ones where he was placed, and began to sing and to tell stories, until I saw my father smiling and talking to him. The car stopped only once on the way to Sharjah, for the afternoon prayer, and we reached Sharjah city that afternoon, pulling up in front of our house and the house of my aunt, my father's second wife. My father ordered the driver 'Abdallah Banderi to take his sister's two sons to their mother, and took me with him together with the Ja'lani and his bodyguard 'Ayyid bin Khusaif to the main *majlis* in our house. We found the house open but empty of people. My father said Salmeen must be there. (Salmeen bin Suwailim was an Omani from Nakhl who had been a slave when my father bought him and set him free; but Salmeen preferred to live with us.) My father called out, 'Salmeen . . . Salmeen,' and I joined in with him: 'Salmeen . . . Salmeen.'

Salmeen appeared, supporting himself on one leg and drag-ging the other as he walked, a result of the paralysis that had struck him when he was young. My father told him, 'Heat up some water so that Sultan [me] can bathe and put it in the bath-room next to the *majlis*.' My father ordered his guard 'Ayyid bin Khusaif to go to the barber shop of 'Isa Namaku and fetch him. After that he took me with him to the house of my aunt, his second wife, where my sisters were and also my younger brother, Humaid. After he had washed and changed his clothes we went to the *majlis*; he had brought with him soap and a towel but when we got there we found that the barber, 'Isa Namakuh, had not arrived. My father looked through the window of the *majlis* that gave onto the square in front of our house, and there was the barber, carrying his case and hurrying, but he couldn't go any faster and was swaying as he walked, like the pendulum of a clock; his legs were bowed outwards. 'Isa . . . You're very late,' my father said. Isa Namakuh replied, 'Greetings, Shaikh Muhammad . . . I was shaving someone and had shaved only half his head – so how could I leave him?' 'Come on,' my father said, 'shave Sultan.'

Namaku put his equipment on the ground and wrapped me up in a piece of cloth. He began to cut tufts of my hair with his scissors – tuft after tuft – and put them in a piece of cloth in my lap. I was grieving over the loss of this hair that I had taken care of and had trained down over my temples like bunches of grapes; how could I face my friends – them with their hair and me bald? I burst into tears. My father said, 'Isa . . . have you injured the boy's head?' Isa said, 'I haven't used the razor, I've just been cutting with the scissors!' After the barber had shaved my hair, leaving me with more than one cut, Salmeen started to wash me in warm water and my father said to him, 'Rub the soap all over his body.' Then my father took me, dried me and dressed me in the garment he picked from the clothes bag I had brought with me; and I wrapped my head in my red shawl.

After the sunset prayer I went with my father to the fort, where my uncle Shaikh Sultan bin Saqr al-Qasimi was in his library. I kissed my uncle on his nose, as my father had advised me, and he clasped me to his chest, sitting me down close to him. No one was in the library other than my uncle and my father; my father explained to his brother Shaikh Sultan what had happened in Ras al-Khaimah and while that was going

27

on one of the guards came in, and said: 'Shaikh Sultan bin Salim al-Qasimi, Ruler of Ras al-Khaimah, has arrived at the door of the fort.' My uncle Shaikh Sultan ordered him to be brought in and went forward to greet him. He came in with his two sons, Saqr and Khalid; my uncle brought them into his library and a family *majlis* council was held. Shaikh Sultan bin Salim al-Qasimi had married the sister of my uncle and my father, so they were maternal uncles of Saqr and Khalid, the two sons of Shaikh Sultan bin Salim al-Qasimi. Shaikh Sultan bin Salim was distraught; he implored my uncle and father to do anything they could to return the rule of Ras al-Khaimah to him.

This was not the first time I had seen Shaikh Sultan bin Salim al-Qasimi, for I had done so a few weeks before when I accompanied my father to visit him in Ras al-Khaimah. On that occasion the Bedouin had gathered in Kharran to protest to my father, explaining that Shaikh Sultan bin Salim was cutting down the well-established *ghaf* trees in the region of Jiri, and especially those whose branches were used for the sterns of Kuwaiti boats (known as *boum*). These Kuwaiti long-distance boats had begun to convert to the use of engines rather than sails and I myself had seen two camels carrying the trunk of a big tree fastened between them. Shaikh Sultan bin Salim refused to listen to my father's advice so my father went back to Kharran and told the Bedouin what had passed between him and Shaikh Sultan bin Salim.

Shaikh Sultan bin Salim told my uncle Shaikh Sultan bin Saqr that his sister, Shaikha Fatima bint Salim al-Qasimi, was in Ras al-Khaimah fort when Shaikh Saqr bin Muhammad al-Qasimi

entered it; she was on the ground floor and shouted in the faces of
the Bedouin, calling them traitors. Shaikh Sultan bin Salim said
that his son Khalid told him of this and he heard of it when he
was in the house of Shaikh Humaid bin Muhammad al-Qasimi.
He also heard that Shaikh Saqr bin Muhammad had ordered
the Bedouin not to enter the ground floor but to confine themselves to the upper floor and the entrance to the fort, in order to
preserve the honour of his aunt.

Shaikh Sultan bin Salim al-Qasimi now wanted to bring his
sister out of the fort, take her to Sharjah and find a solution to
the question of government in Ras al-Khaimah. My uncle Shaikh
Sultan bin Saqr al-Qasimi undertook to go to Ras al-Khaimah
himself to meet Shaikh Saqr bin Muhammad al-Qasimi;
my father promised to write a letter to Shaikh Humaid bin
Muhammad al-Qasimi asking him to get his aunt, Shaikha
Fatima bint Salim al-Qasimi, from the fort in Ras al-Khaimah
and send her to Sharjah. Shaikh Sultan bin Salim al-Qasimi said
that his car was ready to go to Ras al-Khaimah.

My father wrote the letter requested and gave it to Al-Ramis,
the bodyguard of Shaikh Sultan bin Salim, charging him with
handing the letter to Shaikh Humaid bin Muhammad al-Qasimi.
I asked my father if I could go with them and they could drop
me off in the Kharran district for me to visit my mother, which
he agreed to. I sat in the front seat of the car, with the driver
called 'Uqab. Al-Ramis sat in the rear of the car, which was
open, and in the back were some sacks whose contents I did not
know.

After leaving Sharjah in the early evening, Al-Ramis asked me
to move to the rear of the vehicle so that he could sit in the front

seat beside the driver. My small body slipped between the sacks of the load and I fell into a deep sleep. I woke up to the sound of Al-Ramis' voice saying, 'Get up, we are near your house.' The driver, 'Uqab, said, 'Do you see the track of your car? Follow that track and you'll arrive at your house.' I got out of the car and they didn't give me a moment to think before they left me in the middle of the road and went on their way. I looked for the car until its lights were lost among the trees. It was a dark night and the moon had not yet risen because we were in the last days of the lunar month of Rabi' al-Awwal. The distance to our house was one and a half kilometres and there were no houses in that region except the house of my maternal uncle, Salim bin Khamis al-Suwaidi: he was my father's uncle really, but we used to call him uncle. There was also a small house near it that belonged to two ladies, Shaqrouh and Hamrouh, of the Bani Dhawi clan. All of those houses were near the fort at the top of the hill, and I was at the bottom – I had to climb to the top of the hill.

There were wolves howling nearby and fear took a hold of me. One night a few days before, wolves had got into Shaqrouh's sheepfold and taken one of the lambs; I was afraid of suffering the same fate so I started running as fast as I could. I stumbled several times before arriving at our house and called out for my mother repeatedly until she opened the door. She was astonished: 'How did you get here without me hearing the car?' I said, 'They put me down on the main track and I ran from there.' My mother said fervently, 'May God punish them ... the track is full of wolves.' The next day I didn't leave the house so as not to run into my friends with my shaven head. They were a group of Bedouin boys with long hair; the oldest of them was called Mashroom and another was called Al-Za'abi, from nearby Jazirat al-Hamra.

We used to meet up every day: each of us carried a bow made from the stem of a bunch of dates, and an arrow with a needle tied to it, both of which we made ourselves in order to hunt doves and small birds. We used to light a fire with a lighter belonging to Mashroom, by striking the steel on its flint onto dry straw, and then lighting the fire by blowing on it. We would sit around it eating whatever we had caught and roasted – locusts, lizards, jerboas and birds. We went through the fields of rain-fed wheat grown by my father in Salihiyya, near Hail – one of the green knot of villages – using the date-palm stalk to drive away the small birds from the wheat ears.

After a number of days, my father arrived from Sharjah, bringing with him the things he wanted for receiving his brother, my uncle, Shaikh Sultan bin Saqr al-Qasimi. The latter was coming the next day to mediate between Shaikh Saqr bin Muhammad al-Qasimi, who had taken control of Ras al-Khaimah, and Shaikh Sultan bin Salim al-Qasimi, then in Sharjah where his wife (my aunt) 'Aisha was, and Dubai, where his second wife lived. In the morning of the day that Shaikh Sultan bin Saqr al-Qasimi was to arrive, my father was busy setting up the tents and their amenities. At sunset that day Shaikh Sultan bin Saqr al-Qasimi arrived with his retinue and guards at the tents my father had set up near our house. He stayed there that night after the feasting and, on the following day after breakfasting, Shaikh Sultan bin Saqr al-Qasimi got in his car with my father, while his retinue and guards took other cars, and set off for Ras al-Khaimah to meet Shaikh Saqr bin Muhammad al-Qasimi.

At noon my father arrived back from Ras al-Khaimah and told us that Shaikh Sultan bin Saqr al-Qasimi had returned to Sharjah on the coast road. I asked my father about the outcome and he answered: 'No progress.' Days passed and Shaikh Saqr bin Muhammad al-Qasimi consolidated his rule in Ras al-Khaimah. He asked the British to recognise him as Ruler of Ras al-Khaimah, which they did.

In the first week of March 1948 my father decided to visit Shaikh Humaid bin Muhammad al-Qasimi, the brother of Shaikh Saqr bin Muhammad al-Qasimi, the new Ruler of Ras al-Khaimah, in Ras al-Khaimah itself, and he took me with him. While we were there a violent storm blew up that forced my father to stay the night with Shaikh Humaid. Our driver 'Abdallah Banderi and the bodyguard 'Ayyid bin Khusaif slept in the outside *majlis* while I slept with my father in a room inside the house; it was the room of Shaikh Humaid himself. Early in the morning, when the door of the room was opened, I saw that the interior courtyard of the house had become a pool of water. I asked my father what had happened during the night because I had slept through it, so he called to 'Ayyid bin Khusaif to carry me outside the house to see the situation in the city.

As soon as 'Ayyid took me outside I saw that all the houses, most of them made of palm leaves, had been levelled to the ground; the shoreline had come close to Shaikh Humaid's house and you could see the sea from there. There had been three or four palm-leaf houses between us and the sea, which the waves had carried away; the wells belonging to the houses had fallen in and the sea had swept away the sand around them, leaving them standing like pillars along that wide coastline after the sea had stopped its scouring and withdrawn. 'Ayyid and I hurried along the shore to the north; the coast took us towards the *suq* and brought us to the creek. Here, in the north of Ras al-Khaimah town, houses had been demolished by the mighty waves after the violent sea had broken through to Ras al-Khaimah creek.

My father was concerned about his people in the area of Kharran so we got in the car and went there; when we arrived we found our house, composed of several tents, no longer standing. But there were my brother Khalid and the servants coming forward to greet us with smiles on their faces: 'Thank God you're alright,' said my father as he got out of the car. We all went on to the fort, and there was a clothes line here, another one there, and a third one a short way away for women's clothes: all were soaking from the rain.

My brother Khalid told my father what had happened that night. He said: 'We were asleep in the big tent – my mother, my sisters Shaikha and Na'ima, my little brother 'Abdallah and me – when the storm blew up. Suddenly the tent ropes came out of the ground on all sides, leaving the tent supported only on the two central poles. When the tent left us uncovered my sister Shaikha and I ran towards the fort in the pitch dark. When the lightning lit up the sky we found our infant brother 'Abdallah crawling in the sand; we carried him with us to the fort.'

When we went into the fort we were surprised not to find my mother and my sister Na'ima there. I told my uncle Salim bin

Khamis and went with him to search for them in the tent, which was now down and spread out on the ground. My uncle and I were calling for them when we heard voices from underneath the tent, flat on the ground. We raised one side of the tent in order to get to them and there was my mother calling on God. I said to her that 'Abdallah was with us in the fort.

My mother said: 'We had been searching for 'Abdallah under the tent, which was soaking wet and heavy; the more we tried to crawl the more we stuck to the ground. O Muhammad, what a calamity!' My father said, 'All better now, God willing.' My mother went on, 'While we, and the wife of your uncle and her infant, were sleeping in the fort, suddenly muddy water poured down on us from an opening in the fort's staircase. It had been blocked up on the roof and drowned us in a pool of mud.' My father said: 'Let's travel back to Sharjah; gather up your clothes and get in the car. Leave everything – the servants will bring it.' We got into the car on our way to Sharjah, but it broke our hearts to leave that beautiful region behind.

## Opening fire on the British

No sooner had the British recognised Shaikh Saqr bin Muhammad al-Qasimi as Ruler of Ras al-Khaimah than the deposed Shaikh Sultan bin Salim al-Qasimi poured out his extreme anger against them. His activities and intrigues increased to the extent that he received a warning from the British Political Officer in Sharjah in which he was warned that if he did not distance himself from activities that threatened and breached tribal peace he would be asked to live far away from the Trucial Coast, as the British liked to call it. But the British came to the conviction that my uncle, Shaikh Sultan bin Salim, was a choleric individual with whom it was difficult to work, and that it could not be ruled out that he would create problems and raise concerns in the future. Several months later, on 23 July 1948, he was again summoned to the British Political Agency in Sharjah, the seat of the British Political Officer, to meet Mr Cornelius James Pelly, the British Political Agent in Bahrain, who had come to Sharjah on board a British warship.

In the meeting with Mr Pelly, Shaikh Sultan bin Salim put forward several excuses and justifications without any basis, according to Mr Pelly. Mr Pelly asked the Shaikh to accompany him to Bahrain, to which Shaikh Sultan did not object; but when, as the two of them and the British Political Officer went out through the door, Mr Pelly asked Shaikh Sultan bin Salim to get in the car waiting in front of the Agency, the Shaikh refused and stepped backwards. The British Political Officer thereupon ordered his guards at the entrance to the Agency to arrest Shaikh Sultan, who drew out his pistol remarkably quickly and began firing while running away. The shots passed close to Mr Pelly and the British Political Officer, who took cover in the car while the British Political Officer shouted to his guards, 'Open fire on him!' The guards opened fire but shot into the air! Those guards were people of Sharjah, known as the Mazem, who provided most of the guards for the forts, towers and strongholds throughout Sharjah.

My uncle Shaikh Sultan bin Salim covered the distance from the British Political Agency to our house, about a kilometre, running from one lane to another. At our house he encountered my father, who took him to a room on the upper floor whose entrance was near the family quarters and which looked onto the western courtyard in front. It also looked onto the western doorway and the yard of the *majlis*, which another doorway separated from the internal accommodation. It was midday when lunch was served to Shaikh Sultan bin Salim, who was trying with my father to find a means of getting him out of Sharjah.

It was only a little while before the noise of cars echoed around our house; my father looked out of the window of the room that gave onto the front courtyard and saw British troops blocking the house on the western side. My father called to his guards and servants to arm themselves and to lock the doors. One of the servants replied that the British troops had sealed off the eastern doorway that gave onto the courtyard of the fort. There was another doorway on the northern side of the house, called the kitchen doorway, not known by most people, which led to a small yard surrounded by the houses of our neighbours, Maryam bint Sa'adallah, Salim Dhira' and Rashid al-Ghazal. The lanes between those houses were not wide enough for more than one person to pass.

My father took my uncle to the kitchen door and found that the British troops had not yet reached it. He took him out of the house and I don't know what he planned after that because I was watching the British troops concentrating on the square in front of the western doorway, through the window looking onto the front square from the upper-floor room.

I saw the British troops sheltering behind a military vehicle which soon reversed and revealed some bulging sacks piled on top of one another; a line of soldiers loomed over them, with their rifles levelled at the western door of our house. I kept a watch until the sun began to set, and then the military vehicle came forward and hid my view of the soldiers behind the sacks. Finally it set off again, leaving nothing behind but some small piles of sand that had leaked from the sacks.

## *My father's exile from Sharjah*

A few days later my father arrived at the house before midday and asked my mother to pack a suitcase of clothes for him. My mother asked about the journey and he said that the British had decided to take him instead of Shaikh Sultan bin Salim to Bahrain. Mr Pelly was no stranger to Sharjah, having been the British Political Officer in Sharjah a year and a half before, and he knew my father, Shaikh Muhammad bin Saqr al-Qasimi, very well. My father had been opposed to the establishment of the airport in Sharjah in 1931, his wish being that it should be civil and not military. He had removed the markers put in the ground for the setting up of the airport and the British had decided to exile him from Sharjah, but had then accepted the conditions put forward by my father providing for the issuance of a letter guaranteeing the protection of Sharjah's independence and non-intervention in its affairs (see the author's *Sharjah Airport Between East and West*, written in Arabic).

The British asked Shaikh Sultan bin Saqr al-Qasimi, the Ruler of Sharjah, to accept the exiling of his brother, Shaikh

Muhammad bin Saqr, to Bahrain and to deny him any non-essential provisions or supplies, or the means for travel. My father obeyed his brother's order and travelled to Bahrain, accompanied by his oldest son Khalid and 'Umran bin Taryam. He stayed in Bahrain for a few weeks as a guest of Shaikh Salman bin Hamad Al Khalifa, the Ruler of Bahrain; he and his companions then returned to Sharjah.

## Qasimiyyah al-Islah School

During the period when my father was away, in September 1948, the Qasimiyyah al-Islah School received its pupils, and I was among the beginners at the school. I was put in the first class – at that time I was nine years and two months old – because for two years I had spent the winters away in the region of Kharran in Ras al-Khaimah. My father was still exiled in Bahrain so I went to the school on my own. The school was built of palm leaves in the shape of tents and covered in sacking on which tar had been spread to stop the rain coming through the roof. The ground was covered with new mats that had arrived rolled up; as a result, when they were spread out they did not lie flat – parts of them stuck up and we sat on them until they were flat. The pupils in all the classes sat on the ground, except in the fifth class where the older ones sat at desks transferred from the Taimiyya School, near the 'Arsa in the *suq* area.

I saw the pupils from the Taimiyya School one day in the crowded 'Arsa *suq*, the centre of which had changed into a fruit market. The pupils went by in a long column cutting through the *suq*, so I followed them; there they were, squatting down on their heels at the edge of the sea like seagulls, separated a little from one another, clearly defecating.

The Qasimiyyah al-Islah School was originally the home of my uncle Shaikh Sultan bin Saqr al-Qasimi, and when he left it for another house two years before he had given orders for it to be converted into a school with the addition of several classes: there was a need for many classes that the Taimiyya School could not provide. My teacher in the first year was Mr Fadhil; he was a dark-skinned man, dressed in a gown and waistcoat and wearing a head cloth – all of them gleaming white. He had come to Sharjah with Shaikh Sa'id bin Butti al-Maktoum after experiencing some difficulties in Dubai. Mr Fadhil had beautiful handwriting; from him I learnt the first steps in writing. The writing was done on black slate with sticks of stone that were almost all white; among them were sticks of many colours. As regards reading the Qur'an, I had studied with Shaikh Faris bin 'Abd al-Rahman before entering the Qasimiyyah al-Islah School.

The headmaster of the Qasimiyyah al-Islah School was Mr Muhammad bin 'Ali al-Mahmoud. He was a stickler for implementing the school rules, and one day there was a disturbance in the school at break time. Mr Muhammad came in with his stick and ordered the school door to be closed; then he chased the pupils who had stirred up the trouble – they were running ahead of him, with him driving them, and the rest of the pupils running behind. There was general chaos in the school.

At one point, there was much talk in the school of a 'long-tailed star' when a comet with a long tail was seen one evening in early 1948.

When spring came and the temperature rose a little, workmen came and erected sunshades made of palm leaves in front of the classrooms. They were divided by two wooden posts the same width as the main supports so as to form open classrooms. The sounds of the collective reading of the Qur'an or the reciting of odes, and the voices of the teachers presenting their lessons, penetrated those open rooms.

## The illness of Shaikh Sultan bin Saqr al-Qasimi

People didn't know that Shaikh Sultan was ill and he showed no signs of it. I saw him in the spring of 1949 in his *majlis* when a peepshow man was brought in. He had arrived in Sharjah carrying a four-legged box on his back; he put the box on the ground and invited people, one at a time, to look through an opening in it. At the same time, in exchange for a small payment, he turned a handle and made the pictures in the box move. People heard about this man – that he was doing witchcraft – and a number of the town's dignitaries went to Shaikh Sultan bin Saqr al-Qasimi, asking him to expel the man from Sharjah. Shaikh Sultan ordered the man to appear before him, so a guard was sent to bring him to the Shaikh's *majlis*. This *majlis* was in the western house, the home of his wife, Shaikha Mira bint Muhammad. I was with his sons, sitting beside the town's notables, who had made the complaint. In came the man with the box on his back and the Shaikh questioned him: 'What country are you from?' 'From Iraq,' he said. 'And what are you showing in that box?' asked the Shaikh. 'Entertainment for children,' said the man. Then

Shaikh Sultan, my uncle, said: 'Come here, Sultan, you look in the box and tell us what you see.'

The man took his box and put it in the light coming from the *farkha*, a small flap in the closed door, and started to turn the handle. The pictures began to move inside the box and I could see them through the peephole. The owner of the box was commentating on every picture I was seeing in the box: 'This is the large bear; it eats wheat and barley.' He described 'Antara bin Shaddad, the poet-warrior hero of a sixth-century epic romance, and also Abu Zaid al-Hilali, the great tenth-century Arab tribal hero, and then it was finished. My uncle, Shaikh Sultan, said, 'Describe for us what you saw.' So I, only nine years old, stood up in front of the Shaikh and the dignitaries and explained confidently and carefully what I had seen. Shaikh Sultan decided afterwards to send the owner of the box away from Sharjah and to give him some money.

I was sure that Shaikh Sultan bin Saqr al-Qasimi was ailing when I once saw him being given an injection in his forearm by his son Khalid, after boiling the needle. This was after having lunch in the central house, the home of his wife, Shaikha Latifa bint Sa'id. I was sitting beside him while he was eating supper with his sons and saw him adding sugar to the rice; I had never tasted rice with grains of sugar on it, but for the first time I sampled potatoes roasted with fat and they were delicious.

At the beginning of May 1949 the celebrations were held for the marriage of Khalid, the son of Shaikh Sultan bin Saqr al-Qasimi, to my sister Shaikha bint Muhammad al-Qasimi. At that time, as I was one morning leaving my uncle Shaikh

Sultan's house – the one known as the western house, where Khalid's mother Shaikha Mira lived – I saw my uncle sitting on a bench in front of the house. When he saw me he called 'Sultan . . . Sultan' and I walked back to him. He lifted me up and sat me near him; he wrapped me in his cloak and kissed me, and the scent of roses was in his clothes. One of his companions asked him: 'Who's the father of this boy, Shaikh Sultan?' He said, 'This is Sultan . . . son of my brother Muhammad. He's named after me.' Shaikh Sultan took a coin from his pocket and put it in my hand: 'Do you know what this is?' I said, 'It's a rupee.' He closed my hand over the rupee and said, 'Don't lose it or let anyone take it.' My slight body slipped through his hands and I ran back to our house.

The following day all the wedding celebrations were cancelled, and grief was evident on people's faces when news spread in the morning that Shaikh Sultan was ill. The illness had become worse during the previous night, with pains in his lower abdomen. Dr McCaully, Senior Medical Officer in the Gulf region, who lived in RAF accommodation in Sharjah, was called to treat him. Dr McCaully came every day but my uncle's temperature kept rising. Then he was beset by continuous hiccuping. After Shaikh Sultan had been in that state for several days, the doctor advised us to transfer him to Bombay.

My father, his brothers and the sons of Shaikh Sultan bin Saqr al-Qasimi went to Sharjah airport to bid farewell to Shaikh Sultan on his journey to India. He was accompanied by his sons Muhammad, Salim and 'Abdallah, and his maternal uncle, Salim bin Khamis al-Suwaidi. The airfield was crowded with those saying goodbye with tears in their eyes and downcast spirits, their sad voices repeatedly invoking God. My father was on the verge of tears and embraced his brother for a long time on the plane before take-off. Shaikh Sultan bin Saqr al-Qasimi was forty-three years old at the time.

# 3

*Deputy Ruler of Sharjah*

## The accident

IN MAY 1949, AFTER THE journey of my uncle Shaikh Sultan bin Saqr al-Qasimi to India, my father deputised for him in the Emirate of Sharjah. The first traffic accident in that period was the one involving 'Abd al-'Aziz, the son of Shaikh Saif bin Mijlad, the Qadi of Sharjah, and I witnessed it in all its details.

One day, we were sitting and enjoying a game of *qabbah*, a ball game similar to baseball, between the Eid prayer ground in Sharjah and the taxi stand. Suddenly there was the sound of a collision from the direction of the taxi stand, and the people there were gathering around something. Others were running towards the accident, and I was among them. When I got there I found a gap in the crowd and saw a man with his legs broken and blood pouring profusely from them; he was repeating, 'Take care of my children.'

The man was lifted into a car and rushed to Sharjah air-base, where there was a hospital for the British. My cousin

47

Khalid, the son of Shaikh Sultan bin Saqr, had a rifle in his hands and took a car to speed after the vehicle that had struck 'Abd al-'Aziz. He caught up with it after it had got stuck in sand near Al-Hira, a suburb of Sharjah. Its driver, called Yunus, fled and left some women in the car. The car that had taken 'Abd al-'Aziz to the air-base now returned with him: he had died en route to the hospital. It was said that 'Abd al-'Aziz himself had deliberately stepped into the path of the car to stop it, thinking that he was strong enough to do so, while reading some lines of Al-Ghazali, an Omani book of superstitious magical power.

## Summer residence at Sha'am

With the arrival of the summer in 1949, my father took us to Sha'am, situated in the Musandam region near the border between Ras al-Khaimah and Oman, to spend the season there; he went back to Sharjah, since he was deputising for his brother during his absence in India. Sha'am is a small place and is the last in a string of villages belonging to Ras al-Khaimah. It is formed of a narrow, sandy strip on the coast, then a narrow stony plain with some *samr* trees, called *al-ay*, and finally, the high mountains that surround Sha'am from the east and block the coastal strip's extension northwards. It intrigued me that those desolate mountains could produce different kinds of fig: the white variety, which was big and oozed a honeyed juice when fully ripe; another type, reddish black, that was small but sweet to eat and called *suqub*; and also a type of hazelnut called *miez*.

On the southern side was a mountain, detached from the range, that was shaped like a pyramid, and at its summit were ruined buildings: it was known as Jabal Sanam (Idol Mountain). The water in Sha'am was pure and plentiful, from wells on the coast known as *bidaya* (plural *bidi*). Our house, made out of palm leaves, was in the far south, on the coast; it was a hundred metres from the last house in the village, which was the house of Shaikh Saif bin Muhammad bin Mijlad, the Qadi of Sharjah, whose son had been killed in the accident. Shaikh Saif was not the only one spending the summer in Sha'am, for most of the summer visitors were Sharjah people.

Opposite our house a sandy hill sloped down from the foot of the mountain across the stony plain to the sandy beach; it was free of rocks and earth, and was the colour of gold dust. Every morning I would climb to the top of the hill, where there was still shade from the mountain. I climbed barefoot until I came to the very top where it joined the slope of the mountain, and from that towering height I could see the village hidden behind the palm trees, and the white sand of the coast spreading its arms to welcome the waves of the open, limitless sea. Ravens hovered and circled in the air, and I imitated them, raising my arms and running at top speed down the slope of the hill to the beach, with my feet lightly and nimbly skimming the surface.

Our daily pastime was swimming in the sea and using our feet to search for *mahhar*, oysters, buried in the sandy seabed. They were as big as the palm of the hand, and if our feet felt an oyster we dived down and collected it. There was another kind of oyster as well; it was small and was called *hama*. Women used to take these from the coast west of Jabal Sanam when the sea

49

had receded from the islands and revealed the seabed, known as
*hid.* A group of women used to pass our house along the beach
carrying baskets full of the *hama* oysters on their heads, heading
northwards to sell them in the village.

On some days, when the sea became stormy and the waves
rose, we couldn't go down to the sea so we played on the beach,
boys and girls together. We put empty tins on the edge of
waves as they collapsed and receded from the beach, and then
ran to pick them up before the waves could swallow them. On
one occasion, one of the daughters of Shaikh Saif bin Mijlad
wasn't able to recover her tin when it went faster than her, so
she followed it. A wave approached with its wide-open mouth
and she tried to retreat towards us, but the wave closed over her
and the sea swallowed her up. The girl could swim, but the
current swept her away. Her brother Nasir, who was older than
us, flung himself into the rolling waves and managed to grab her,
but the current took them both away from the beach. We could
see nothing except a black gown floating on the water, appearing
and disappearing with the waves.

A great shout went up from boys and girls, and everyone
came out from the neighbouring houses; Shaikh Saif bin Mijlad,
the father of the girl, arrived and I saw him standing on the
beach, leaning on his stick and raising his face to the sky as he
called on his Lord to save his daughter. Suddenly, a muscular
young man rushed up and threw himself into the surging waves;
he was a resident of Sha'am called Hammud, who worked for
Shaikh Saif bin Mijlad. In the distance we could see two figures
coming closer together until they met, and everyone cheered
with joy. People celebrated still more when they saw the two

figures getting closer to the shore, as the situation became ever clearer: the young man had hitched Shaikh Saif's daughter and her brother onto his back and was swimming with both arms against the current. Finally, he dropped them onto the beach and threw his exhausted body down beside them. That was a time of joy for everyone who had come to the shore.

## My school

After the summer season had finished, we returned to Sharjah. The Qasimiyyah al-Islah School opened its doors for the school year 1949–50 (this was the school built of palm leaves) and most of the pupils plus all of the teachers attended. But the headmaster of the school, Mr Muhammad bin 'Ali Al Mahmoud, had been transferred to Qatar, to teach there, and had been replaced as headmaster by Mr Mubarak bin Saif al-Nakhi. I was admitted to the second class of the school which was now without the older pupils, who had finished their school studies. In June 1950, after I had finished my studies in the Qasimiyyah al-Islah School, we received news that Shaikh Sultan bin Saqr al-Qasimi had completed the last of his operations in the Indian hospital and was talking about a date for his return to the country after the end of Ramadan 1369 – that is, July 1950.

My father bought the farm belonging to Salim bin Sultan bin Salim al-Qasimi (the son of the Ruler of Ras al-Khaimah), and the house attached to it in the village of Ghubb in Ras al-Khaimah. Salim bin Sultan al-Qasimi had been deputising for his father in Ras al-Khaimah at the time of the coup in 1948 and fled by boat from Ras al-Khaimah to Sharjah, where he settled. My father took us to Ras al-Khaimah in the summer of 1950 to spend the summer season there; he stayed with us for a few days and then went back to Sharjah. He had to go back because he was deputising for his brother as Ruler and preparing to welcome him when he returned from India – but he never returned.

We went back to Sharjah after spending the summer in Ras al-Khaimah and saw that the Qasimiyyah al-Islah School, built of palm leaves, had been replaced by a building made of blocks of coral and gypsum. It had been Isma'il al-Buraimi's house, a well-known merchant in Sharjah who had dealt in folk medicines and maintained the register of births in the city. He used to register the name and the date of birth of a newborn when the family came to buy medicinal herbs and other remedies from him. My uncle, Shaikh Sultan bin Saqr al-Qasimi, had bought the house from Isma'il to replace the palm-leaf school whose roof leaked like a sieve when it rained.

The replacement school had five classrooms for boy students and another, with a palm-leaf curtain, for the girls, plus a room for a library. The school year was 1950–51 and there were many changes in the school: the name of the school was changed from the Qasimiyyah al-Islah School to the Qasimiyyah School; there was now a class for girls and a library with a few books. The pupils of the fifth grade had graduated from the school and their place was taken by the successful pupils from the fourth grade. New students joined the school in the first grade and I was among those in the second grade who passed into the third grade.

The headmaster, Mr Mubarak bin Saif al-Nakhi, had not yet arrived at the school for the new school year. We were told that he had moved to Qatar to teach there, and that Mr Ahmad bin Muhammad Abu Ruhaima was to be the new headmaster.

Towards the end of 1950, I met an artist from India while I was walking in the market on my way to one of the shops. The artist told me that he had a 'BA'. I didn't know what that meant. He said he was a painter and that he would paint for me anything in exchange for the price of a ticket on the steamship to India. I took the painter with me to my father and told him what the man had said. I suggested that the man paint on the walls of the private upper rooms in our house.

My father liked my idea, and wrote a letter for me to the owner of the shop in which paint was sold. We bought some tins of paint in different colours and some brushes.

The painter painted pictures on the walls of the room. I helped him paint the pictures, which made the room bright and attractive. When my father saw the pictures on the walls of his room, he gave the painter some money to help him get back to his country.

## Bandits

In addition to his duties as the representative of his brother during his absence, my father was also responsible for the security of Sharjah. At that time, attacks by bandits had increased, and the last attack had taken place only two miles from Sharjah. Rumours spread about the arrival of Major Richard Hankin-Turvin, an officer of the Arab Legion in Jordan. Word had also got around that the British were going to recruit military units from among the citizens of Sharjah. In order to settle any doubts he had about this, my father requested a visit to the British forces in the Royal Air Force camp. He did not, however, get the opportunity to see Hankin-Turvin.

My father invited the Political Officer from the British Agency in Sharjah, Patrick Stobart, to our house for a lunchtime banquet. He tried to get him to discuss the question of the military recruiting and the arrival of an Englishman in Arab military uniform.

My father said angrily, 'The bandit attacks will not cease as long as the British government restricts its interests to the coast and gaining full control of that area alone. They have failed to take control of the interior regions.'

My father managed to arrest one of the bandits who had been pillaging the cars passing through the desert and kidnapping children to sell into slavery. He jailed that bandit in the prison in the Mahlusa, inside the fort. I went with my father to see him.

The door of the Mahlusa prison leads from the inner courtyard behind the gate called *al-Isbah*, where the greatest concentration of guards was located. When we passed by it to the inner courtyard of the fort we were not disturbed by the voices of the prisoners there. The door of the prison was at the end of the narrow walkway. In such a space, a person could not make out the shape of the door because of the pitch dark. Nothing from inside the prison could be heard due to the thickness of the wooden door. I stood with my father in front of the door, and the guard unlocked a big lock. When the lock was opened, the guard pushed the two thick doors inwards. My father entered, and I followed him with the guard. The place was dark except for a faint light coming from the ceiling of the prison, and it had a terrible stench. We approached a man who was hanging upside down by his legs. There was pole in the ground, and he was hanging from the top of it. He was completely naked except for a loincloth, and his hands were tied firmly behind his back. He had defecated down his back, and faeces had caked on the back of his head. He had also urinated down his stomach and chest, and urine permeated his beard. He was repeating over and over, 'Kill me, Shaikh Muhammad! But don't torture me!' My father replied, 'I will make you an example to others.'

My father ordered him to be taken out of the prison and sent to his people, but when they went to put him in the car he wasn't able to go because he was so weak and thin.

## The death of Shaikh Sultan bin Saqr al-Qasimi

At the beginning of 1951, the doctors advised Shaikh Sultan bin Saqr al-Qasimi to go to London to be treated by specialists in the urinary tract and rectal surgery. His condition was very complicated as he had a serious disease affecting the area between the bladder and the large intestine. He underwent five operations, but without satisfactory results after treatment lasting eighteen months.

On Thursday 8 February 1951, Shaikh Sultan bin Saqr al-Qasimi left Bombay for London on an Indian National Airlines plane to receive treatment there. He was accompanied by his sons Khalid and Muhammad, and a medical consultant whose name was Dr K. M. Masani. When he arrived at Heathrow airport, he was checked into the London Clinic.

News arrived that there would be a noticeable improvement in the health of Shaikh Sultan after just one month of treatment in the hospital. All the members of the family and the residents of Sharjah rejoiced at the news.

However, on 23 March 1951, Shaikh Sultan bin Saqr al-Qasimi passed away suddenly after an operation in the London Clinic. He was forty-five years old. It was decided that he would be buried in Sharjah.

## Shaikh Muhammad bin Saqr al-Qasimi, the Ruler of Sharjah

My father, Shaikh Muhammad bin Saqr al-Qasimi, was the representative of his brother Shaikh Sultan bin Saqr al-Qasimi for the two years of his absence for treatment in India and Great Britain. He had been his brother's Deputy since the beginning of his rule in Sharjah, and had been in charge of security, and was the person Sharjah looked to in times of crises. Following the death of Shaikh Sultan bin Saqr al-Qasimi, rule in Sharjah was transferred to my father. This took place on 23 March 1951. On Saturday 24 March, he received crowds of mourning citizens who came to express their condolences on the death of his brother.

The following day, my father wrote letters to a number of rulers and Shaikhs, informing them that he had succeeded his late brother, Shaikh Sultan bin Saqr al-Qasimi, as the Ruler of Sharjah.

In the evening of 26 March, Shaikh Saqr bin Sultan al-Qasimi, the late Shaikh's son and my cousin, went to meet Mr John

Wilton, the British Political Officer in the British Political Agency in Sharjah. Saqr claimed that his uncle had succeeded by way of deceit, and that a devious plan had been concocted by Shaikh Sultan bin Salim al-Qasimi (the past Ruler of Ras al-Khaimah) and the Midfaʿ family (the family of Ibrahim al-Midfaʿ, the Minister of the Ruler of Sharjah) against the wishes of the Qasimi family and the people of Sharjah.

Mr Wilton replied that Shaikh Muhammad had succeeded in a natural and harmonious way. He asked Shaikh Saqr if he had any evidence to substantiate his claims. Shaikh Saqr replied that this was common knowledge, and that all he asked for was justice, as was his right. He said that it was unacceptable that the Midfaʿ family should receive all of the riches of the country while the children of Sultan and his family were just getting by.

Mr Wilton said that if this were true, and if Shaikh Muhammad bin Saqr al-Qasimi had succeeded Shaikh Sultan against the wishes of his family and the people, why then had the British not heard of the family taking any steps to let this be known to the general public?

Shaikh Saqr replied, 'They are afraid of Shaikh Muhammad. He spread a story with the help of Shaikh Sultan bin Salim al-Qasimi that the Trucial Oman Levies [a newly established British-Arab Legion patrol force] would quell any resistance to their plan.' Mr Wilton replied that the Levies were not for installing Shaikh Muhammad, or any other person, in power.

He asked once more if Shaikh Saqr could show any solid evidence to support his claims.

Shaikh Saqr said, 'The family will write a letter to you saying that they want Saqr, and not Muhammad, to be their Ruler.'

As soon as Shaikh Saqr bin Sultan al-Qasimi left the British Political Agency, the voices of armed troops could be heard that evening in the different districts of Sharjah as they called on the residents to go to the fort the next day, Tuesday 27 March 1951. They announced, 'O people of Sharjah . . . You are requested to go tomorrow morning to the fort to pledge your allegiance to Shaikh Muhammad bin Saqr al-Qasimi as the Ruler of Sharjah.'

On the morning of 27 March, the people crowded in front of the fort to congratulate Shaikh Muhammad on his accession to power. At the same time, Shaikh 'Abdullah bin 'Abdul-'Aziz al-Najdi arrived at the British Political Agency. He was an elderly man who lived in Buraimi. There he met Mr John Wilton, the British Political Officer.

Mr Wilton said that Shaikh 'Abdullah al-Najdi had repeatedly told him the same story that had been told to him by Saqr the day before. He also made certain insinuations about the character of Muhammad bin Saqr and Sultan bin Salim. He advised Mr Wilton to expel the latter individual immediately.

Mr Wilton said that he had pointed out to al-Najdi that Shaikh Sultan bin Salim had been present for the funeral of his cousin. Al-Najdi replied: 'All right . . . But get rid of him as quickly as possible. When this has been done, you will find that the matter will be resolved.'

The British disliked Shaikh Sultan bin Salim al-Qasimi, as he had opened fire on Mr Pelly, the British Political Resident in Bahrain, and on the British Political Officer in Sharjah. They knew that Shaikh Muhammad bin Saqr al-Qasimi was a strong man who opposed many of the things done by the British.

However, Wilton said that he personally felt that Muhammad might prove to be a strong ruler, and that Sultan would not be able to urge him to act in any wicked and malicious way, it not being in Muhammad's nature to be violent. That is, any wicked things that might take place when he was the Ruler would be a result of his weakness in responding to such acts, and not for any other reason.

On the morning of 28 March 1951, the Qasimi family – old and young – gathered, led by Shaikh Muhammad bin Saqr al-Qasimi, the Ruler of Sharjah, in the upper chamber and in the walkway in front of it. Shaikh Sultan bin Salim al-Qasimi, the previous Ruler of Ras al-Khaimah, was present, as was Ibrahim bin Muhammad al-Midfa', the Minister for the deceased Shaikh Sultan bin Saqr al-Qasimi. Also present was the British Political Officer, Mr John Wilton, to pay his respects.

On the following morning, the entire family was again present, as were Shaikh Sultan bin Salim al-Qasimi and Ibrahim al-Midfa'. Also present once more was the Deputy British Political Agent, to convey the respects of the Deputy British Political Agent in Bahrain, C. J. Pelly. Ibrahim bin Muhammad al-Midfa' stood up to give a eulogy in which he praised the late Sultan bin Saqr. He concluded his talk with the hope that Shaikh Muhammad would follow the same path of sincere cooperation and fruitful friendship with the Government of His Majesty the King of England, as characterised by the reign of his brother.

When the British Deputy left, Shaikh Muhammad bin Saqr al-Qasimi asked him to convey his gratitude to the Deputy British Political Agent in Bahrain, Mr Pelly, for his message of condolence. He also asked him to convey his sincere desire for cooperation with the British government in all matters.

Shaikh Saqr bin Sultan al-Qasimi was present at all the events. He expressed his grief to the British Political Officer, and asked a question about the return of the body of his father for burial.

In London, the body of the deceased was washed, wrapped and placed in a coffin in preparation for the journey to Sharjah. On 30 March 1951, Khalid bin Sultan and Muhammad bin Sultan, the sons of the late Shaikh Sultan bin Saqr al-Qasimi, arrived at the London Clinic to collect the body of their deceased father. This was to be flown from London to Sharjah on board a plane chartered for them by the Iraq Petroleum Company, which had the oil concession in Sharjah.

The general public referred to Iraq Petroleum as 'Lermitte', the name of the company's director. Khalid and Muhammad were accompanied by an Arab named Munir Shamma, who was an employee of the BBC's Middle East Service, and was acting as a translator. He was to return on the same plane to London. At the farewell to Khalid and Muhammad, the sons of the deceased Shaikh, was C. M. Rose, the Desk Officer for the Gulf in the Eastern Department of the British Foreign Office in London. He had been responsible for the deceased Shaikh and his two sons in London during the period of the Shaikh's treatment. He informed Khalid and Muhammad about the recruitment of the Levies (the local soldiers), and that Sharjah had been chosen as the location of their headquarters (since the air-base was there).

Rose was asked by the British Resident in Bahrain to ask Khalid, the son of the deceased Shaikh Sultan, about the issue of succession. He replied, 'When I asked Khalid about this issue, he confirmed that his uncle was to be the one to succeed his father as Ruler. He also told me that there was no problem regarding the elder brother taking over from the father, as the issue had been decided based on the wishes of the general population.'

He had a low opinion of Saqr, but a high opinion of his uncle, as he was in the end to succeed his father.

## The burial of the deceased

News arrived that the plane carrying the body had taken off from London for Sharjah.

On the morning of the second Monday of April 1951, the plane carrying the body of the deceased, Shaikh Sultan bin Saqr al-Qasimi, arrived at Sharjah airport. Khalid and Muhammad, the sons of the deceased, came down the steps of the plane, followed by Munir Shamma. My father embraced his nephews, who were crying, and my father was shedding tears, too. I stayed close by my father's side.

The body was transported in a shiny, brown wooden coffin with bronze handles on its sides. It was placed in an open-topped military Land Rover and was driven from Sharjah base to the Grand Mosque. The body had been washed and shrouded in London according to Islamic rites, and it was now taken from the coffin and laid on a bier. Then prayers were offered for the deceased, and the bier was carried on shoulders to the Jubail Cemetery. Crowds of people followed the funeral, among them the brothers of the deceased and their children, and myself, our eyes filled with tears. When the body arrived at the cemetery where the grave had been prepared and was taken from the bier, it was noticed that blood had leaked from it; I myself saw it in the abdominal area.

The body was lowered onto the area in front of the hole that had been dug for the grave. My father got into the grave. He and those with him began loosening the cords that held the shroud together. My father bent over the body, weeping. When the burial rites had been completed, the crowds of people went back to the fort to offer their condolences.

It was a dull day and the southern wind, the *suhaili*, was blowing lots of dust. There was a belief among the people that a dusty day was a day of misfortune, and indeed it had been.

## *The power struggle*

After the funeral and the burial rites had been completed, Mr Wilton, the British Political Agent in Sharjah, wrote the following in a letter to his counterpart in Bahrain:

> When I returned from Dubai on Monday, 2 April, after the visit of His Excellency the British Resident in the Gulf, I found that the funeral rites had been completed in the morning. Khalid and Muhammad had accompanied the body of their father from London. They had wasted no time waiting for my arrival with Saqr. They expressed their surprise that Saqr had not succeeded to power (after his father) yet, and that they desired no other solution than for him to do what he must do.

He also said that Khalid appeared to have changed his mind since he had spoken to Rose. Initially, Khalid was not sure that

Saqr would treat him well, but later Saqr cunningly promised him that he would be his crown prince. Mr Wilton, the British Political Agent in Sharjah, sent a letter to Shaikh Muhammad bin Salim al-Qasimi, the father of Shaikh Saqr, the Ruler of Ras al-Khaimah, asking him to act as a mediator between the two sides in the dispute in Sharjah.

On Thursday 5 April 1951, Shaikh Muhammad bin Salim al-Qasimi arrived in Sharjah and met Mr Wilton at the British Agency in Sharjah. He asked for his advice about arriving at an agreement to resolve the dispute upon which all could agree.

On Friday 6 April, Shaikh Muhammad bin Salim al-Qasimi shuttled between Sharjah Fort, where Shaikh Saqr bin Sultan al-Qasimi resided, the home of Shaikh Muhammad bin Saqr al-Qasimi, and the home of Shaikh Majid bin Saqr al-Qasimi, where the uncles of Shaikh Saqr had gathered. They were the brothers of Shaikh Muhammad bin Saqr al-Qasimi: Shaikh Majid, Shaikh Humaid, Shaikh Rashid and Shaikh Khalid bin Khalid al-Qasimi.

On 7 April, Shaikh Muhammad bin Salim al-Qasimi met Mr Wilton at the British Political Agency in Sharjah. He told him that both sides insisted on a number of points:

1. Shaikh Saqr bin Sultan al-Qasimi would accept nothing less than his immediate appointment as successor to his father.

2. Shaikh Muhammad bin Saqr al-Qasimi spoke of retiring after one or two years, but insisted that he would not do so at the present time.

3. The uncles were not able to find a solution to the problem of succession. Shaikh Muhammad bin Salim al-Qasimi suggested to Mr Wilton that the uncles go and discuss the issue

with him. After some indecision among the uncles, they set a time for Thursday 12 April 1951.

Seven anxious days went by in Sharjah. Shaikh Saqr bin Sultan al-Qasimi and his brothers were gathered in the fort, while Shaikh Muhammad bin Saqr al-Qasimi and his brothers were at the house of Shaikh Muhammad, my father.

On Thursday 12 April 1951, at the British Agency in Sharjah, at exactly half past nine in the morning, Shaikh Majid, Shaikh Humaid, Shaikh Rashid and Shaikh Khalid bin Khalid gathered for the meeting with Mr Wilton. By the end of the meeting, all of them had declared that the matter would be referred to the British government for a decision. Mr Wilton decided to call all members of the Qasimi family to the British Political Agency in Sharjah.

In the early morning of Friday 13 April 1951, all the members of the Qasimi family came to the British Political Agency in Sharjah, with the exception of the two rivals. They met Mr Wilton, who told them that the decision must definitely be made by them and not by any other party. Then he left them with Shaikh Muhammad bin Salim al-Qasimi to try to arrive at a decision. By the time of the noon prayer, they were still unable to come to any solution except to say that they wanted the Ruler to be one who could prove his worth.

Mr Wilton wrote in his letter to the British Political Resident in Bahrain: 'If the family votes strongly in favour of Saqr, and Muhammad will not budge from his position, I am not sure how we could proceed with the matter. I think that in such circumstances we must formally recognize Saqr and reject any dealings with Muhammad. Muhammad may accept this without the use of force from our side.'

On 14 April 1951, Shaikh Saqr bin Sultan al-Qasimi realised that not one of his uncles would commit himself to anything, and that the family conference might delay the matter indefinitely. He went to the British Political Agency in Sharjah and met Mr Wilton. He asked him if the British government would mind if he went on a tour to gain the support of prominent men in the community, and the extent to which Mr Wilton was prepared to listen to their wishes.

Mr Wilton replied that there would be no objection to this. He assured him that he was prepared to listen to their opinions regarding the issue of succession, and that he truly would like nothing better than to know the wishes of the general population.

On Sunday 15 April 1951, Shaikh Saqr bin Sultan al-Qasimi contacted a number of prominent men in the town. He asked them to go to the British Political Agency in Sharjah and to cast their vote for him. This continued over the next two days.

By Monday 16 April 1951, Shaikh Saqr bin Sultan al-Qasimi's attempt to solicit the views of the people of Sharjah was clearly bothering Shaikh Muhammad bin Saqr al-Qasimi. There was much confusion among the people, to the detriment of the reputation of the Qasimi family. That night, he went to the house of Mr 'Ali al-Bustani, who was the Assistant to the British Political Agent, to try and persuade him to intervene in the matter as an intermediary between him and Shaikh Saqr in the negotiation of his allowances if he withdrew. However, 'Ali al-Bustani favoured the idea that the matter be discussed with Shaikh Muhammad bin Salim al-Qasimi.

## *Shaikh Saqr bin Sultan al-Qasimi, Ruler of Sharjah*

In the morning of Tuesday 17 April 1951, my father, Shaikh Muhammad bin Saqr al-Qasimi, summoned his brothers to his house and convened a closed meeting with them.

My father told us:

My brothers were asked to leave their weapons and come with me to the Sharjah Fort to meet with Shaikh Saqr bin Sultan al-Qasimi. At the front gate of the fort, the door was not opened until the guards there were certain that we were unarmed. They were watching us from the two slots through which anyone who tried to break through the gate would be shot. As the gate opened we found Saqr standing in front of it on the inside. As soon as he saw me, he exclaimed, 'Uncle!' He kissed me, and kept saying that he would not go against my authority. At that moment I was certain that Mr 'Ali al-Bustani had told him about my decision to back down.

My father said, 'We sat with Saqr, and I said to him, "This rule was reinstated by force. Don't think that it is the British who will make you the Ruler; I am the one who will make you Ruler. Do the things that you are able to do, but if you face any difficulties refer back to me and to your uncles to solve them."'

My father said that Saqr kissed him and his uncles after they had given him their blessing as the Ruler. As my father was telling us what happened, the cannons in front of the fort fired five shots. When he heard this, Shaikh Muhammad bin Salim al-Qasimi rushed to our house. Then he went outside and entered the fort, and from there went to Mr Wilton at the British Political Agency in Sharjah. He was carrying letters from my father, Shaikh Muhammad bin Saqr al-Qasimi, announcing his resignation and his withdrawal in favour of Shaikh Saqr bin Sultan al-Qasimi, and a letter from Shaikh Saqr bin Sultan al-Qasimi announcing that he was to be the Ruler. He was twenty-eight years old at the time.

On Wednesday 21 May 1951, we went out of the Qasimiyyah School and into the front courtyard of the fort, where we raised the flag of Sharjah. We were headed by the headmaster of the school, Mr Ahmad bin Muhammad Abu Ruhaima, and the teachers. We found a tent had been set up in front of the gate to the fort. The headmaster arranged us in lines from east to west in front of the fort. In front of us were white lines on the ground which formed a division between us and the tent. When men of the Royal Air Force arrived in Sharjah along with the Levies, they took us to the gate of the fort and made us line up parallel to the fort.

The ceremony for the British recognition of Shaikh Saqr bin Sultan al-Qasimi as the Ruler of Sharjah took place as follows:

1. The placing of the escorts of the Royal Air Force and the Levies in front of the fort on three sides of the lined field, where there were seats for the Rulers and a group of Europeans in a tent that had been erected.

2. The arrival of the Political Resident in the Gulf with his companions, and their taking their seats.

3. The departure of Shaikh Saqr from the fort, his passing through arches of palm branches, and his welcome. This was followed by inspection of the guards, and then a welcome by

the British Political Resident in the Gulf, who accompanied him until he was seated to the right. Then the entourage took their seats in the right side of the tent.

4. A speech by the Political Resident in the Gulf, in which the British government recognised the succession of Shaikh Saqr bin Sultan al-Qasimi as the Ruler of Sharjah after his father.

5. A speech by Shaikh Saqr bin Sultan al-Qasimi, the Ruler of Sharjah, in which he pledged to honour the agreements signed between the British government and his father.

6. The departure of the Political Resident and his companions, with appropriate salutes.

7. The entrance of His Highness the Ruler into the fort, with the appropriate salutes.

My father avoided those festivities. He also avoided the *majlis* of Shaikh Saqr bin Sultan al-Qasimi in the fort following an incident that occurred when a man came to make a complaint. The man sat down in front of my father and proceeded to voice his complaint. Suddenly Shaikh Saqr bin Sultan al-Qasimi yelled at the man, 'I am the Shaikh, not him! Come over here!'

At the end of May 1951 the Qasimiyyah School in Sharjah closed for the holidays. My father took us to Ras al-Khaimah to spend the summer in the region of Ghubb. I had at the time finished the recitation of the entire Qur'an with Mr Fadhil; there was a custom that whoever completed the recitation of the Qur'an would provide lunch for the teachers and students of the school.

In the region of Ghubb in Ras al-Khaimah, my older sister, Shaikha bint Muhammad al-Qasimi, got married. This had been delayed for two years because of the sickness and death of my uncle, Shaikh Sultan bin Saqr al-Qasimi. The bridegroom was his son Shaikh Khalid, who had accompanied his father during the period of his treatment in India and Britain. My father spent the entire summer with us in Ghubb, in Ras al-Khaimah.

4

*The Development of*
*Education in Sharjah*

EDUCATION IN SHARJAH AT THAT time went through five stages:

## Stage 1: The school year 1951–52

When we returned to Sharjah after having spent the summer in Ras al-Khaimah, we entered the Qasimiyyah School (now at the house of al-Buraimi). It was September 1951, and I was in grade four. I had a new teacher, Mr 'Abdullah al-Qaiwani, who had taken the place of Mr Fadhil. The headmaster of the school was Mr Ahmad bin Muhammad Abu Ruhaima. A few days after we had started grade four, the new headmaster came in with a thin young man. He presented the man to us saying:

This is Mr Nasr Al-Ta'i. He has been appointed as the English teacher for grades four and five. As grade five has only a small number of students and there is a large number in grade four, some of you will join grade five. This will fulfil the number of students required for grade five.

Mr Nasr tested the students one by one until it was my turn. I went up to the blackboard and he dictated the following verse to me:

*If the man has not had his reputation tarnished by being mean-spirited, whatever he wears is beautiful.*

The oral test concluded, the headmaster and the English teacher left the grade four class. I was the only student who went with them to join the grade five class.

All the students in grade five were older than me. They had all studied arithmetic before me, which was used in business at that time. The class teacher, Mr Ahmad Abu Ruhaima, designated one of the students, Muhammad Habib al-Yusuf, to explain basic arithmetic to me, which he did very well.

The English teacher, Mr Nasr al-Ta'i, was severe in his treatment of the students. All of the students had received punishment from him except me. I was treated well. Because of the small number of books available, one book had to be shared between two students. Student A, who lived in the south of Sharjah, might share with student B, who lived in the north of Sharjah. Whenever Mr Nasr asked student B about something in the book, the response would be, 'It is not in my half.' This sentence was repeated over and over throughout that lesson. Eventually Mr Nasr asked why the students kept talking about 'my half'. Student B replied, 'I am from the north of the city and he is from the south, so how can we do our homework together? For this reason, we divided the book into two, and unfortunately my half does not cover the topic we are studying.'

One morning in November 1951, Shaikh 'Abdullah al-Salim al-Sabah, the Emir of Kuwait, visited Sharjah. In the *majlis* of my cousin Shaikh Saqr bin Sultan al-Qasimi, the Ruler of Sharjah, Mr Ahmad Abu Ruhaima presented a student, Taryam bin 'Umran, to give a welcoming speech to Shaikh 'Abdullah. In the speech, he made a request on behalf of the students in Sharjah for books and teachers for the school.

When Shaikh 'Abdullah al-Salim al-Sabah left the gate of the fort, he saw a row of students from the fifth grade being led by Mr Ahmad Abu Ruhaima. Before he got into his car, he leant towards us. With him was Shaikh 'Abdullah al-Jabir al-Sabah, the Minister of Education in Kuwait. He said, 'Teacher, your request has been forwarded to Shaikh Abdullah al-Jabir al-Sabah.'

That was the start of a joyous day. The students and teachers waited happily in great anticipation for what was to arrive from Kuwait. The books in our library would come to us from Egypt via India, and the shipment from Egypt to Sharjah by sea used to take a number of weeks.

On a December morning in 1951, after the students had gone to their classes, the headmaster, our class teacher Mr Ahmad Abu Ruhaima, was told that the grade three teacher, Mr Fadhil, was absent.

Mr Ahmad Abu Ruhaima asked us, 'Do any of you know where Mr Fadhil's house is?'

I answered, 'I do. He lives near my house.'

The headmaster said to me, 'Go and ask him why he didn't come to school today.'

I said to him, 'He prayed the dawn prayer with us today.'

I left the school and went to the house in which Mr Fadhil lived. The door to his house appeared to be shut, but when I gave it a push it opened. The door to the only room in Mr Fadhil's house was open. I went inside, where I found him leaning against the wall, his legs stretched out in front of him. His eyes were wide open, staring straight at me. I called out to him, 'Mr Fadhil! Mr Fadhil!' But there was no response. I grabbed one of his legs and shook it. But he did not move.

'He's dead! Mr Fadhil is dead!'

I burst into tears on my way to the school. I kept repeating, 'Mr Fadhil is dead! Mr Fadhil is dead!'

When I found Mr Ahmad Abu Ruhaima, my first words were, 'Mr Fadhil is dead!'

The headmaster jumped up and summoned the teachers, and they went to the house where Mr Fadhil lived. They washed his body, wrapped it in a shroud and took his body to the 'Bedouin Mosque', which was in front of the Qasimiyyah School. The teachers, students and other people prayed for Mr Fadhil following the midday prayer that day. After that, the body was taken for burial. The students were excused from school for the rest of the day.

In March 1952, an education delegation from Kuwait visited the Qasimiyyah School in Sharjah. The delegation was led by Yusuf al-Fulaij, who was a well-known merchant in Kuwait. They had come to observe the level of education in the school and the number of students there. A welcoming ceremony was held for the delegation in which poems were recited and speeches were made. Mr Nasr al-Ta'i wrote a speech in English for me to present, and those who were there were delighted by it.

In April 1952, the English teacher, Mr Nasr al-Ta'i, was dismissed for unauthorised behaviour. Whenever a student had made a mistake with him, he tied the student's legs and beat them severely with a *falaqa*, a kind of wooden bar to which the student's legs were tied and then raised up. The student was then beaten on the soles of his feet. Another kind of punishment involved a student being given two pieces of coral from the sea to hold up high while squatting on the ground. Yet another involved putting a slate board - the kind used by the students to write on – on the chest of the student and another on the student's back; the boards bore the words, 'I am lazy. Look at me and laugh.' If the punishment was severe, the words were, 'I am a donkey. Look at me and laugh.' The student would be paraded in front of the classes with these words, and all the students would laugh and make fun of the student being punished.

Mr Nasr had also decided to forbid the use of Arabic language in the classroom during English lessons. He decided that students should speak only English. Whoever spoke Arabic would be given a special circular piece of wood, and two annas (one anna equals one-sixteenth of a rupee) would be taken from him. One anna would be given to the previous student who had held the piece of wood, and the other anna would be put in the money box. Whenever a student said anything in Arabic, the students would call out, 'Give him the log!'

As this was the first time that English had been taught in the school, students would communicate with each other using sign language. On one occasion, Mr Nasr al-Ta'i asked the students about the meaning of an Arabic word in English. One of the students in the final row raised his hand and eagerly waved his index finger, urging the teacher to let him answer. Nobody else raised their hands in the class, and so all the students turned to look at that student. He then made a sign in sign language. He put his index finger on his chest to signal the meaning 'I'. Then he pointed his index finger and middle finger down, and moved them back and forth next to each other to mean 'go'. Finally, he put his thumb on his index finger, and waved them back and forth from his lower abdomen to mean 'urinate'. The students burst into laughter! One of them advised, 'Laugh in English!' and he was punished for that. Mr Nasr al-Ta'i once punished Su'ud bin Sultan al-Qasimi, a student in the fourth grade, by hitting his hands. Su'ud complained about Mr Nasr to his brother, Shaikh Saqr bin Sultan al-Qasimi, the Ruler of Sharjah, and explained to him what was going on in the school. For that reason, Mr Nasr al-Ta'i was removed from the school and expelled from Sharjah.

A few weeks of the term were left at the Qasimiyyah School. The Assistant British Political Officer at the British Political Agency in Sharjah, Martin Buckmaster, gave up his time to give English lessons at the school in the evenings. However, this did not continue. He was replaced by Jasim bin Muhammad bin Jasim, who at that time was an employee at the British Political Agency in Sharjah. But he didn't last long either. That was when the school was about to close for the summer holidays at the end of May 1952.

We spent the summer holiday in Ras al-Khaimah in the area of Ghubb. We had staying with us that summer Matar Fairuz, who had returned from Riyadh. He had been studying *fiqh* (Islamic jurisprudence) in one of the institutes there.

Matar Fairuz was a young orphan boy. He had been afflicted with smallpox at the end of 1935 when it had spread through Sharjah and the other emirates. It was decided to put him in quarantine, with other people suffering from smallpox. This place was called the *mujadder* ('place of smallpox'). When my father found out about this, he asked that Matar be brought to our house. My mother was worried for her children, but my father said, 'This small boy has lost his eyesight. Who would we leave him with at the *mujadder*? I will attend to his medical needs myself.'

My father treated the boy until he recovered from the disease. My older sister Shaikha was given the task of taking him to the school of Faris, the Qur'an teacher, and bringing him home again. He attended the school until he had memorised the entire text of the Qur'an. My father then sent him to Riyadh to complete his studies at an institute for Islamic studies.

In Ghubb, Matar was housed in the *majlis*, which was a sort of hut with a palm-branch roof. I got used to taking him early every morning, holding his hand and walking with him over long distances. Sometimes we would walk, and other times we would hurry along. I was his eyes to see with. He would tell me stories about the life of the Prophet Muhammad and some of the traditions about the Prophet. Sometimes he recited verses of poetry, most of them proverbs and words of wisdom.

## Stage 2: The school year 1952–53

When I returned to the Qasimiyyah School in Sharjah, I found that many things had changed.

Firstly, the headmaster, Mr Ahmad bin Muhammad Abu Ruhaima, had left the school to travel to Saudi Arabia.

Secondly, the students were different. Some of the previous students had joined the army of Trucial Oman (the Trucial Oman Scouts), which had been established by that time. Others had joined the British at their base. Taryam bin 'Umran and his brother 'Abdullah had left to be with their relatives in Kuwait and to study in the schools there. Muhammad bin Hamad al-Shamisi had moved to Bahrain to study there. He lived in the central part of Bahrain.

The student 'Ali bin Muhammad Abu Ruhaima, the brother of the headmaster of the school, Mr Ahmad bin Muhammad Abu Ruhaima, was the oldest student in our class. He became the teacher of the grade five class, which consisted of students who had been transferred from the fourth grade. I was among those students, and I came back alone to join my classmates.

The teacher, Mr Ali Abu Ruhaima, had begun writing the first play in the Qasimiyyah School, entitled *The Firewood Collector and the Sultan's Daughter*. He also acted in it.

The building for the Qasimiyyah School had been bought by Shaikh Sultan bin Saqr al-Qasimi from Isma'il al-Buraimi, as I said earlier. After the death of Shaikh Sultan bin Saqr al-Qasimi, the building was inherited by his widow, Shaikha Mira bint Muhammad al-Suwaidi. Now, she demanded that the building be given back.

There was a large building in the Shaikhs' Quarter which belonged to Muhammad bin 'Ali bin Kamil. His daughter, the mother of Salim bin 'Abdul-Rahman al-Midfa', had passed away in this building and Muhammad bin Kamil subsequently abandoned it for another house. The new Shaikh, Saqr bin Sultan al-Qasimi, bought Ibn Kamil's house and the Qasimiyyah School was moved to it. The girls' section was moved to the northern part of the house after it had been divided off with a wall of palm branches.

The new headmaster of the school, Mr Isma'il, had been brought from Bahrain. He made the older students in the school wear short trousers. He walked around with them in the streets of the city of Sharjah, and held sporting activities in the evening in front of the city's residents, who rushed to see them. The more conservative residents of Sharjah protested, some of them threatening to take their children out of the school. So Mr Isma'il advised that the students should not continue the activities in the evening, and that the sports activities should be held in the school during official working hours.

At the beginning of 1953, two ladies arrived in Sharjah from Oman. One of them was Sarah Hossmann, who was an elderly woman with a wooden leg, and the other was Maryam Khatoon. They were from the American Mission in Oman, and were renting the house of Al-Sirkal from my father. They converted the house into a maternity hospital, and it came to be known as 'Sarah Hossmann's Hospital'. Most of the children in Sharjah born at that time were born at that hospital.

When the Qasimiyyah School closed for the summer holidays, my father took us, as usual, to the area of Ghubb in Ras al-Khaimah. This time, my father was late in returning to Sharjah. The people warned him, 'The town disapproves of those who come back late.' That is, a person who spends a long time away from his town will be cursed with a fever. The general population didn't know why that happened, but my father knew that it was because of the mosquitoes which had spread everywhere at that time, and so he took the necessary precautions.

When we stayed longer this time in Ghubb, we were told that there was to be a festival called Nayruz. To the general population this meant 'the end of the season'; that is, after the dates which had dried on the tree were collected. They were spread out on the hard ground, and then sorted and left exposed to the sun. That place was called the *mustah* (spreading floor). After a few days, they were put in bags made of palm leaves. A small bag was called a *jirab*, and a large one a *jilla*. These were sealed and put in a dark room with the door tightly shut so that insects and rodents wouldn't be able to get in. That room was called the *mudbbasa* ('syrup maker'). The large bags were piled up and laid out against the channels underneath, and the pressure and heat caused syrup to drip from them into the channels. The syrup was then collected in pots placed on the floor of the *mudbbasa*.

Nayruz would begin with a bullfight. The owners of the plantations brought their bulls, which were normally used to drag buckets of water to irrigate their farms. Families came from everywhere to the flat area just in front of the Shaml area. They chose bulls of similar sizes to fight each other. The bulls butted each other until one of them was defeated, and then two more bulls were brought forward. My brother Saqr brought one of the bulls from our farm. It was large in size and had two curved horns. My brother had sharpened its horns with a file until they had become as sharp as two spears, a practice that was prohibited during Nayruz. A young bull with small horns was brought forward to face my brother's bull. The owner of the bull was Saif al-Ramas. The two bulls faced each other and began butting each other with their horns. My brother's bull broke the rules and slashed the bull of Saif al-Ramas with one of its sharp horns, leaving a neck wound that went from its ear down to its shoulder. The bull belonging to Saif al-Ramas flew into a rage and butted my brother's bull in the stomach, which caused the bull to drop to the ground. The other bull continued butting it all over its body. My brother's bull got back up and fled from the battle. The bull of Saif al-Ramas followed it until my brother's bull entered our farm. The bull of Saif al-Ramas followed it inside, and the two bulls fought each other throughout the night.

## Stage 3: The school year 1953–54

When we returned to the Qasimiyyah School in the house of Ibn Kamil at the beginning of September 1953, the Qasimiyyah School in Sharjah came under the administration of the Department of Education in Kuwait for the 1953–54 school year.

At the beginning of September 1953, two teachers arrived who were sent by the Department of Education in Kuwait; they were Mustafa Taha, to be the headmaster, and a teacher, Mr Ahmad Qasim al-Boraini.

The headmaster and the teachers set tests to determine the levels of the students. The result would constitute the basis for the division of classes from the first up to the fourth grade. At that time, the first school football team was established.

The levels were also set among the female students in the girls' school. The headmaster taught along with a local woman who was the Qur'an teacher.

83

For the summer holidays we travelled to our farm in Ghubb. My father was with us at the time with his military escort, called Saif al-Dahh. He slept on the ground in front of the outer *majlis*. Once he got up and ordered the second escort, named Mas'ud, to shoot at the palm trees in the plantation with his rifle. My father jumped up, and rushed with his sons over to Mas'ud. When my father asked him why he had fired his gun, Mas'ud replied, 'Saif al-Dahh ordered me to do it.'

My father enquired, 'What were you shooting at?'

Mas'ud replied, 'The sail that was passing through the centre of the farm.'

My father asked, 'Did you see it?'

Mas'ud responded, 'No, but Saif al-Dahh told me about it.'

My brothers Saqr and 'Abdul-'Aziz and I were certain that this had been planned by Saif al-Dahh to scare us. He had been trying to collect almonds which had fallen during the night. He did this after the dawn prayer, from the large tree that had smooth branches and which nobody could climb. It had big leaves and its fruit was as large as the palm of my hand: it wasn't the variety of almond that was well known in Syria, but a local tree common to Bahrain. We decided that we would go to the farm before Saif al-Dahh got there to bathe in the pond at night. When we saw him coming, I hid with 'Abdul-'Aziz behind the trunks of the palm trees. Saqr dived into the bathing pond, leaving his face just above the surface of the water.

Saif al-Dahh arrived at the pond, which was enveloped in darkness. When he slipped into the pond, Saqr submerged himself and grabbed his legs under the water. Saif screamed loudly and pulled most of his body out of the pond except for his legs, which Saqr then grabbed and held onto. Saif screamed again, louder than the first time, and got himself free of the pond. He began running along the path which led to the gate of the farm; from there he ran onto the open land, and from there to the *majlis*. He was completely naked.

In the morning, when we sat with my father around the breakfast table, Saif al-Dahh was talking about what had happened to him the previous night. He said, 'His fingers were like saw blades but I hit him, and defeated him. Then he ran away from me.'

Sitting beside Saif al-Dahh was my brother Saqr. With him was a bundle of clothes that Saif had left behind the night before. When Saif spoke, my brother prodded him. Signalling with his head, he prompted Saif to look behind him. When Saif saw the clothes, he shut his mouth.

Soon news spread there that there were *jinnis* in the plantation of Shaikh Muhammad bin Saqr al-Qasimi, in Ghubb. People became more certain of this when I brought two scary masks with me from Sharjah. I put one of them on, and then I came out from under the aqueduct as people passed by. Some of them responded by fleeing in terror, while others reacted by threatening me with a knife, at which point I fled.

One day, a man came to the village selling lemons on a donkey with a foal. The lemon-seller brought some lemons to give to the maid who worked in our house. I slipped off the saddlebag of lemons with my friend Rashid bin Sultan al-Makhawi. We both climbed up onto the donkey and put on our masks. I was at the front of the donkey and at the back was Rashid, facing backwards and holding the donkey's tail. Then we rode into the eastern quarter of the village of Ghubb. When we arrived, the women started screaming and rushing away carrying away their children. The other children followed us amid the billowing dust and the screams.

## Stage 4: The school year 1954–55

At the beginning of September 1954, Mr Muhammad Dhiyab al-Musa, a Palestinian, arrived from Kuwait to take up a position as a teacher in the Qasimiyyah School.

In November of the same year, Mr Muhammad Dhiyab al-Musa collected Scout uniforms and equipment and formed the first Scout group in the emirates. This was in Sharjah, and the group came under his leadership. The First Sergeant was Sultan bin Muhammad al-Qasimi – me!

In January 1955, the first Cub Scout group was established in the emirates, also in Sharjah. It was delayed because some of the items necessary for its establishment had taken a long time to arrive from Kuwait. The leadership of the Cub group went to Mr Ahmad Qasim al-Boraini (another Palestinian teacher), and the Cub Master was Sultan bin Saqr al-Qasimi, the son of the Ruler of Sharjah.

At the girls' school, which was attached to the boys' section, the teacher Sharifa, also Palestinian, arrived to start teaching the girls.

The students of the Qasimiyyah School moved to a new building, built in the style of a school, halfway between the city of Sharjah and the British base. The house of Ibn Kamil was converted into a school for girls at the end of the 1954–55 school year. In the summer holidays in June 1955 I travelled with my family to the Kingdom of Saudi Arabia to perform the Hajj pilgrimage. A description of this journey appears in the next chapter.

## Stage 5: The school year 1955–56

That year, Mr Muhammad Dhiyab al-Musa was promoted to the position of headmaster. An Egyptian delegation arrived, consisting of Mr 'Abdul-Rahim Muhammad and Mr Gharib 'Abdul-Salihin. A new student, Muhammad bin Hamad al-Shamsi, joined our class. He had been studying in Bahrain. Also joining the students were Taryam bin 'Umran, 'Abdullah bin 'Umran bin Taryam and Sa'id 'Ubaid al-Sha'ir, who had all come from schools in Kuwait.

An annual sports festival was held, and the Scouts in Sharjah took part in the Scout Camp held in Kuwait.

## The participation of the Scouts in Sharjah at the 10th Scout Camp in Kuwait

At the beginning of 1956, Mr Muhammad Dhiyab al-Musa, who was the Scout Master and headmaster of the Qasimiyyah School, decided that a group of the Sharjah Scouts would take part in the 10th Scout Camp in the Funaytis region of Kuwait. It was called the 'First Jamboree', and was held on 15 March 1956. The Sharjah group comprised:

- Myself, First Sergeant, Sultan bin Muhammad al-Qasimi, Group Leader
- Scout Master, Sa'ud bin Sultan al-Qasimi, my cousin

- Scout, Humaid bin Nasir al'Uwais
- Scout Master's Assistant, Salim bin Ibrahim al-Mazru'
- Scout Master's Assistant, Bayyat Muhammad al-Huraiz

In order to make us look smart, Mr Muhammad Dhiyab al-Musa appointed me to buy material to be made into 'suits' for the members of our group, and to purchase shirts, shoes, socks and underwear. I took the members of the group with me to the market and bought everything they needed. The passports were ordered by Sa'ud bin Sultan al-Qasimi.

On 12 March 1956, Mr Muhammad Dhiyab al-Musa took us to Sharjah airport and handed me the passports, Scout flags, flags of Sharjah and some money. He advised us to be on our best behaviour, telling us that we should represent our country and our school in the best way possible.

We travelled on a Gulf Air plane to Bahrain airport, and from there we flew to Kuwait, arriving just after midday. A representative of the Department of Education in Kuwait greeted us there. With him was Salim bin 'Abdullah al-Mahmoud, who had been educated in Kuwait.

From Kuwait airport, a car took us with the representative of the Ministry of Education and Salim bin 'Abdullah Mahmoud to Kuwait City. We were taken to 'Orient House', where Salim bin 'Abdullah al-Mahmoud and some students from the Trucial emirates who were studying in Kuwait were staying. They housed us in a large room with five beds.

On the next day, Salim bin 'Abdullah al-Mahmoud took us on a tour of important places in Kuwait. We visited the wall of Kuwait, the gates to the city and other landmarks in the town.

The following morning we put on our Scout uniforms, packed our bags and got into the car that would take us to Funaytis. When we arrived there, we saw written at the top of the large gate, 'Scout Camp Ten – First Jamboree'. On one side of the gate the names of the different groups participating in that camp were written. There were sixteen groups, which were as follows:

- Thanawiyyah Scouts
- Mubarakiyyah Scouts
- Sharjah Scouts
- Siddiq Scouts
- Fintas Scouts
- Mirqab Scouts
- Failaka Scouts
- Salahuddin Scouts
- Sharqiyyah Scouts
- 'Umariyyah Scouts
- Shamiyyah Scouts
- Muthanna Scouts
- Al-Fuhayhil Scouts
- Sabah Scouts
- Jahra Scouts
- National Scouts

Decorations and flags were hung for the opening of the Camp on 15 March 1956.

When we arrived at the Scout Camp, we were guided to our campsite. We were surprised to see Ahmad Qasim al-Boraini, who had been a teacher at the Qasimiyyah School in Sharjah and was now the leader of the Cub group there. He received us in his capacity as the Scout Master at Al-Fuhayhil School. We shared a single campsite with them.

We received our tent and the tools needed to set it up from the management of the camp, as well as mattresses, blankets and sheets. We pitched our tent straight away, and raised the flag of Sharjah.

That evening, we took part in the rehearsal for the opening ceremony, which was to take place the following day. Another rehearsal took place the following morning.

That afternoon, Shaikh 'Abdullah al-Jabir al-Sabah, Director General of the Department of Education in Kuwait, was received by Mr 'Abdul-'Aziz Husain (Director of Education), Mr 'Isa Ahmad al-Hamad (Leader of the Camp) and Mr Hasan al-'Ali (Deputy Leader of the Camp).

Shaikh 'Abdullah al-Jabir was seated on a chair in the shade of a large tent, and then the parade began. Every group in the camp passed in front of Shaikh 'Abdullah al-Jabir al-Sabah.

When the parade finished, a semicircle was drawn on the ground in front of Shaikh 'Abdullah al-Jabir al-Sabah and all the Scouts in the camp were seated on the line of the semicircle.

The ceremony began with a speech by Mr 'Abdul-'Aziz Husain, Director of Education, and a speech by the Camp Leader, Mr 'Isa Ahmad al-Hamad. Immediately after that, the master of ceremonies made the following announcement: 'And now, a speech from the Sharjah Scouts, presented by Sultan bin Muhammad al-Qasimi.'

I stood up and made an impromptu speech, thanking His Highness, Shaikh 'Abdullah al-Salim al-Sabah, the Ruler of Kuwait, Shaikh 'Abdullah al-Jabir al-Sabah, the Minister of Education in Kuwait, and Mr 'Abdul-'Aziz Husain, the Director of Education in Kuwait. I conveyed our deep gratitude for the teachers, books and stationery they had provided. I said at the end of my speech, 'Whoever has taught me a single letter of the alphabet, I am their slave . . . so what then do I owe to those who have taught me so many words over a period of years?!' Shaikh 'Abdullah al-Jabir al-Sabah called me over and sat me down next to him. He asked about my cousin Shaikh Saqr bin Sultan al-Qasimi, the Ruler of Sharjah.

When the speeches had ended, each contingent gave a performance showing off their different skills until it was the turn of the Sharjah Scouts. Bayyat bin Muhammad al-Huraiz, from the Sharjah Scouts, gave a very impressive performance. He put his legs around his neck, and then started walking on his hands. Shaikh 'Abdullah al-Jabir was so amazed that he got up from his place and went over to Bayyat al-Huraiz, who had given the performance.

When the parade concluded, Shaikh 'Abdullah al-Jabir al-Sabah went on a tour of the camp. He visited our campsite with leaders of the Scout Camp.

After the opening ceremony, pictures were taken in front of the tent of the Sharjah Scouts for us to remember the camp. The pictures contained members of the group from Sharjah and the group from Al-Fuhayhil, as well as Scouts from the emirates who were studying in Kuwait.

There was a supply centre for the camp, where the fresh and

dry food was distributed. It was taken by the Scouts in their boxes to their bases. The Scouts cooked for themselves.

The evening was a good time for enjoying chatting, reciting songs and poetry and holding traditional dances.

One night, a storm descended on Kuwait and the rain poured down. I was a member of the emergency team, and so when I heard the sound of the emergency whistle I rushed to assemble with the other members of the team. We got tools for digging and other pieces of equipment for cutting, as well as ropes, and we rushed to the area where the tents had fallen to the ground. This had happened because the Scouts had not fastened the tent poles and pegs in the ground properly, due to the hard ground in Funaytis. I struck the ground with a crowbar three times, but only a small amount of the hardened sand broke loose. The night was very dark, and so it was hard to see anything. I swung the crowbar down into the hole, unaware that Salim bin 'Abdullah al-Mahmoud, from the Scouts of the Kuwaiti schools, was there, with his hand in the hole. Fortunately, the crowbar missed his fingers, which were clenched in a fist just as the crowbar came down. We set up many tents that night.

There were trips to some special areas in Kuwait. The most important of these was to Al-Rawdhatayn, which is an area of flat land covered in thick grass.

When the Scout Camp in Funaytis ended, we returned to Kuwait City. There we stayed in Orient House for two days, waiting for the plane to take us back to Sharjah.

We flew from Kuwait by Gulf Air to Bahrain airport, and from there to Sharjah.

## *The English private school*

At the beginning of the 1954–55 school year, I was told that an Indian man had opened a private school in the 'room' of 'Abdul-Rahman al-Midfa'. This 'room' was on the second floor of a building on the bank of the Sharjah Creek. One evening, I went there and met the man, who told me that his name was D. S. D'Silva. He said that he worked in the morning at the Locust Control Station in Sharjah writing reports, and in the evening he taught English to students at that school/room.

Soon I joined the English classes and the number of students increased there, forcing Mr D'Silva to ask us to look for another place with a number of rooms. We eventually found the *majlis* of 'Isa bin 'Ubaid al-Nabuda which D'Silva rented for his 'private school'. At that school we learnt how to write letters to companies and reports on different topics that our teacher suggested to us. D'Silva also bought a number of typewriters and we learnt how to type using them.

In the morning, we went to the Qasimiyyah School, and just after midday we went to the private school. When we heard the call to the afternoon prayer, we went to pray in the large mosque near the private school. One day, D'Silva asked us why we went out from the school every day at a set time. We told him that we were going to the mosque to pray.

He said, 'Take me with you.'

I said, 'You are a Christian, not a Muslim!'

He was silent, and didn't say anything else on the matter.

That was until one day when he saw me sitting by myself away from the other students. He came and asked me to explain

Islam to him. Just a few days later, he declared that he wished to become a Muslim.

I said, 'To become a Muslim, you must be circumcised.'

He responded, 'I am all right with that.'

I said, 'Tonight.'

'What time?' he asked,

'After all of the students have left, and the cook Husain Kaidi has gone home.'

'I will let Husain Kaidi finish work at sunset,' he said.

I went to the market, where there was a barber shop and circumciser, whose name was 'Ali Duqlah. I asked him to wait for me and not shut his shop until I came to take him to a house where the circumcision would take place.

After the sunset prayer, I went to one of my neighbours, Khalifa bin Muhammad al-Hadhari, who was the same age as me. I told him what had been arranged, and asked him to come with me to help with the operation. We took the barber, Duqlah, to the private school. We went into the bedroom of D'Silva and found him standing there.

'Where is the boy?' asked the barber.

I said, 'There is no boy. It is this man.'

'Goodness me!' exclaimed Duqlah. 'This one?! Impossible!'

D'Silva was a tall man, while the barber Duqlah was short and advanced in years.

I told Duqlah, 'Don't be afraid. We will tie him up for you.'

The barber said, 'If he kicks me, he'll break my bones.'

'Take off your underwear and sit on the ground,' I told D'Silva.

D'Silva did as he was told. I tied my *kufiya* (headscarf) to his right leg and bound it to his left hand behind his back. Khalifa

94

did the same to D'Silva's left hand and leg, binding it to his right hand behind his back. We tied the ends of each of the *kufiyas* firmly, pushing our knees against D'Silva's back.

I said to the barber Duqlah, 'Put your trust in God, and start.'

The barber performed the circumcision and then dressed the wound. We pulled D'Silva onto a mattress on the ground, and he was as peaceful as a baby lamb.

The barber wrapped up the piece of cloth he had spread on the ground for the circumcision and removed the instruments he had brought with him. We left with him, shutting the door on D'Silva.

Early the next morning, I went with Khalifa al-Hadhari to the private school. When we got close to the bedroom of D'Silva, we heard a moaning sound. We went in and found him exhausted. He had not slept that night. We brought him some breakfast. He asked us to go to the Locust Control Station to tell them that D'Silva was sick, and to request leave for one week.

We treated D'Silva with very basic methods, just as had been done following our own circumcision when we were little. I brought a quantity of goat dung which was one year old. I dug a hole in the yard of the school and lit a fire in the dung that was in the hole. I said to D'Silva, 'Put your circumcision wound into the hole.'

'What? Have you gone mad?' he replied. 'There's a fire in that hole!'

I said, 'It well help it to recover quickly.'

'But I'll burn!' he responded.

I advised him, 'At a distance, and above the smoke only.'

After he did that, his wound healed up.

D'Silva embraced Islam, and started to learn how to pray and read the Qur'an. One day he said to me, 'I want to pray in the mosque.'

I put Arab clothes on him and took him to the mosque for the Friday prayer. We prayed two units of prayer, in which I raised my voice so that he could follow me, and then we sat down in the third row.

The Imam delivered the sermon and the prayer began. When we bowed down, he didn't hear anything from me, and so he said to me in English, 'Raise your voice. ' But as I could not speak during the prayer, I remained silent. When we stood up straight again, he said to me again in English, 'Raise your voice.' Once more I didn't reply. In the middle of the prayer when we were prostrating, he repeated, 'Raise your voice.' When I sat down, he sat himself down in front of me, grabbed my shoulders and protested, 'We didn't agree to do it this way!'

I couldn't contain my laughter so, to avoid disturbing the other people near the end of the prayer, I jumped over the lines of the worshippers and ran away. Behind me D'Silva was calling out to me in English from between the lines of worshippers in the mosque, 'Wait, wait, wait!'

That was the first and last of any prayer performed by D'Silva!

After the completion of the school year, arrangements were made for the purchase of typewriters to improve D'Silva's school. He had resigned from his position so that he could devote himself to his school. That school was now based near the house of Muhammad bin Hamad al-Shamisi, who had returned from Bahrain, where he had been studying, in order to join the Qasimiyyah School in Sharjah, for the 1955–56 school year.

Some money was collected from the students to buy the type-writers. It was Muhammad al-Shamisi who collected the money and went with D'Silva to Dubai to purchase the typewriters. In the Dubai market, D'Silva and Muhammad al-Shamisi became separated in the crowd, and neither of them knew where the other had gone.

After the sunset prayer, I went to the school of D'Silva. I was still learning how to use the typewriter. The person who finished his turn on the typewriter wanted to leave so I could take his place but I said to him, 'D'Silva is drunk. Don't leave me by myself.'

He said, 'How do you know?'

I said, 'I went to drink some water, and I found him with someone else drinking alcohol in his room.'

The lesson was at night, with chairs and tables set out in the yard of the school. Suddenly Muhammad al-Shamisi arrived. When D'Silva saw him, he began to scold him. Muhammad al-Shamisi responded. Their voices grew louder and continued over a long time. They disturbed their neighbours, who included 'Umair bin 'Abdullah al-Falasi, who told Shaikh Saqr bin Sultan al-Qasimi, the Ruler of Sharjah, about the matter.

Minutes later, there was a knock at the door of D'Silva's school. I went to open the door, and there were two of the Ruler's soldiers. They had orders to expel D'Silva from the city. I promised them that I would take him out of the city the next day.

The next morning, I rented a car. D'Silva put his furniture in it and went to Dubai. After a few weeks, we heard a news item: 'A man fell from the third floor of a building, and died. Apparently his name was D. S. D'Silva.'

5

*Hajj*

My father decided to visit his daughter, Shaikha bint Muhammad al-Qasimi, in Dammam, Saudi Arabia. She had followed her husband, my cousin, Khalid bin Sultan al-Qasimi, on 15 November 1954, when he left Sharjah after a disagreement between him and his brother, Shaikh Saqr bin Sultan al-Qasimi. My father was accompanied by my mother, grandmother, my older brother Khalid, my younger sister Na'ima and my youngest brother 'Abdullah. I went with them, along with the servant of my grandmother, called Mubarak.

My father also decided to send us on the Hajj pilgrimage after visiting my sister in Dammam.

## Bahrain

At the end of June 1955, we boarded a British India Steam Navigation Company ship at noon from Sharjah to Bahrain. The ship seemed to be as large as a village. On board I could smell the fresh Indian fruit that had been imported into Sharjah.

I could also smell the smoke emanating from the kitchen, whetting the appetites of the passengers. There were two classes of passengers on board: those who slept in air-conditioned rooms and those who took the much cheaper option of sleeping on the ship's deck.

We slept that night in the air-conditioned rooms due to the stifling heat outside, and the next day we arrived in Bahrain where we were received as guests of Shaikh Salman bin Hamad Al Khalifa, the Ruler of Bahrain. Our hosts took us to the Muhammad Nur Hotel, which overlooked the fruit and vegetable market. We woke up to the sound of the vendors. I asked my father for permission to go to the market; he told me not to be late as the car that would take us to the *majlis* of Shaikh Salman bin Hamad Al Khalifa would be coming.

After I left the hotel, I asked for directions to the Mu'ayyad Bookshop, and people directed me until I got there. I went inside and saw that it was filled with books piled on shelves from the ground to the ceiling. My eyes were so busy looking at all the books that I didn't notice the man sitting on a chair nearby. In front of him was a table. He called out to me: 'What are you looking for, boy?'

I turned to him. He was a very old man. I greeted him and asked, 'Are you Al-Mu'ayyad?'

He replied, 'Yes. What do you want?'

I said, 'I am your penfriend, Sultan al-Qasimi from Sharjah.'

He asked me, 'How old are you?'

'Sixteen,' I replied.

He then asked, 'What do you do with the books you buy, and the other books that I give you as gifts?'

'I read them,' I replied.

I told Al-Mu'ayyad my story with books:

When my uncle, Shaikh Sultan bin Saqr al-Qasimi, died in London, a week went by before his body arrived in Sharjah. While we waited, we sat with the son of the late Salim bin Sultan al-Qasimi in the room attached to his father's library in the western house.

Salim was older than me, as was his brother 'Abdullah, my brother 'Abdul-'Aziz and our cousins. They amused themselves by playing cards. I read books in the library. I perused their titles, memorising the names of the important works of literature which my uncle Shaikh Sultan used to read. Among them were *Al-Shawqiyat* by the poet Ahmad Shawqi, *Literary Gems* and *The Book of Animals* by Al-Jahiz, in which my uncle had written at the beginning: 'This book should not be read.' I didn't read a single sentence of that book. I also looked at some letters, and on some of them was written the name 'Mu'ayyad Bookshop'.

Then Al-Mu'ayyad asked me, 'How are you related to the late Shaikh Sultan bin Saqr?'

I replied, 'He was my uncle.'

He shook his head as if to say, 'Now I understand!'

I went on:

I was gathering some money that was given to me in coins and I changed them into paper notes. I enclosed them in a letter and sent them to you to buy books, whose titles I had remembered, such as *Al-Shawqiyat*, *Literary Gems* and *The Book of Animals*. After I had read the last one, I was certain that it should not be read by a young person. I also bought other books from you: about 'Antara bin Shaddad and Abu Zaid al-Hilali, *A Thousand and One Nights*, and others.

I would read stories to my friends when it was study time, or when I went to some of our neighbours' houses.

Al-Mu'ayyad said, 'This bookshop is yours. Take whatever books you wish and consider them gifts from me to you.'

I thanked him and said, 'I'm in a hurry now as I'm going with my father to the *majlis* of Shaikh Salman. I will come back another time.'

We entered the *majlis* of Shaikh Salman, which was filled with his guests. When my father came close to him, the Shaikh stood up and greeted him with a smile. My father, my brother Khalid and I were given a place to sit that was close to Shaikh Salman. His *majlis* was full of activity: someone would come and say a greeting, while another would bid farewell and leave. This all done in loud voices that everybody could hear, and Shaikh Salman would reciprocate. When the *majlis* was quiet, Shaikh Salman asked his guests one by one how they were, no matter if they were far away over by the door or right next to his chair.

That evening I paid a second visit to the Mu'ayyad Bookshop. This time there was a big crowd. Al-Mu'ayyad sat me down on a chair and sent for a glass of tea for me. Then he gave me a set of books. I thanked him for his gift and asked if I could leave them with him as I would be returning to Bahrain after performing the Hajj pilgrimage.

The following afternoon, my father took us to Rifa' to bid farewell to Shaikh Salman. Rifa' is far from Manama, the capital city. We were received by his two sons, 'Isa and Khalifa, who were riding horses when we arrived. They sat with us on a large wooden seat until their father arrived. Then the Shaikh began a long conversation with my father. I don't know what they talked about, but the two men had been friends since 1948, when my father was exiled by the British to Bahrain, and Shaikh Salman insisted that he stay as his guest. After that, Shaikh Salman bade my father farewell in the same way that he had greeted him.

## Dammam

On the afternoon of the fourth day of our visit to Bahrain, we took a plane to Dhahran airport in the Kingdom of Saudi Arabia. Shaikh Khalid bin Sultan al-Qasimi, my sister's husband, greeted us upon our arrival and took us to the guest house in Dammam.

The road from Dhahran to Dammam was paved. On the western side of the road was white sand, bordered by large tamarisk trees. When we entered the city of Dammam, we encountered soft, golden sand, called *a'dama*. This is where the house of Shaikh Khalid bin Sultan was located, and the guest house was nearby.

The next morning of our visit to Dammam, my father took us to visit the Emir, Su'ud bin Juluwi, the Governor of the Eastern Province. The Emir's *majlis* was calm and quiet. The movements were measured and the voices came in whispers. The Emir sat perched on his chair, his beard covering most of his face. We didn't stay seated for very long, as we left with the Emir's brother, Prince Sa'd bin Juluwi, who was real fun.

During the time we spent in Dammam, I visited my former teacher, Mr Ahmad bin Muhammad Abu Ruhaima, who was working in Dammam.

After spending a few days on our visit to Dammam, preparations were made for us to undertake the Hajj pilgrimage as guests of the Saudi government.

## Jeddah

All of us travelled except for my father, who stayed behind in Dammam. In the morning we boarded a Saudi Airlines plane at Dhahran airport to fly to Jeddah. The planes belonging to that company were twin-engined.

After take-off, our plane travelled safely until we reached a mountainous region on the last quarter of the trip. Then suddenly one of the two engines stopped, and the plane continued flying on only a single engine. It veered left and right. It plunged downwards and then flew up again. The steward told us to fasten our seat belts, and then came out to inform us, 'The temperature of the second engine is rising . . . say your prayers . . . the plane is going down!'

We saw one of the pilots grab the steward by his shirt from behind, pulling him into the cockpit and closing the door. Everyone prayed, and some vomited onto the floor of the plane.

Then the second engine stopped and the plane descended towards the ground. The mountains got closer and closer. The vomit was like a river flowing past us until it collected in a pool around the front seats. From the windows we noticed flat ground beneath us. The plane struck the ground, scraped it and then lifted off again . . . then hit the ground again and scraped it again. Finally, the plane came to a stop.

The steward opened the cockpit door and called out, 'We made it! We made it!'

One of the pilots got out of the plane with the steward and I went with them. We were on a track in the mountains. Then a car came, a red pickup. It was carrying barrels of water. The pilot asked the driver, 'Where have you just come from?'

The driver replied, 'From Al-Muwayh. I am carrying water for the mine at Zhulm area [the old name of the area], the gold mine.'

The steward asked the driver of the car to give him some water, as the water on the plane had run out. The water in the barrels on the back of the car was very hot as it was the middle of the day. There was no food on the plane except for some salty cheese and a little bread.

The second pilot was busy contacting a plane to come from Riyadh airport and land on this track. We had to fix up the track which had been eroded by rain.

The men got out and the steward took out a rubber mat from the floor of the plane. We piled stones on it and then dragged it to the place the captain wanted to fix up. It took us a few hours to flatten out the track. One of the pilots asked each person to give him the white *ghutra* (head cloth) he was wearing. We gathered them all together and he wrapped every *ghutra* around a small rock. Then he laid them straight down each side of the track. In this way, he made signs for a new airport!

The plane from Riyadh landed safely and opened its doors. The steward on that plane said, 'We have seven seats. We have made these available for the guests of the government, as they have children.'

My grandmother, my mother, my sister Na'ima and my brother 'Abdullah were taken off the first plane. My brother Shaikh Khalid and I helped them disembark. But when we all got on board we couldn't find a seat for Mubarak.

The steward said, 'I counted them, seven seats. One of the people from the other plane must have boarded this plane! I will get a list of passengers.' I pointed, and the steward knew that the person sitting to my right was the one who had got on the plane. He then asked the passenger to get off the plane. The response of the passenger, after he had fastened his safety belt, was to hold the clasp with both hands. He said, 'By God, even if you cut me into pieces, I will not take this belt off!'

My brother Khalid said, 'We will leave Mubarak with the men who are in the damaged plane.'

Our plane took off from the runway we had built, on which we had placed our *ghutras*. We flew away, leaving behind what later on became an airport, named the 'Zhulm area airport'!

The passenger who was sitting to my right was the same person who had been sitting to my right in the first plane that had broken down. At that time, he had been watching the right-hand propeller that had stopped, covering his face with both his hands and crying. Now he was looking at the propeller of the plane we were on. He couldn't see the propeller blades because they were rotating so quickly, and he smiled.

We got out at the airport in Jeddah and from there we went to the Basatin Jeddah Hotel.

The hotel consisted of several villas and a range of rooms between groves of ornamental trees and flowers. It was located at the edge of the city of Jeddah, near the water distribution centre which was called Al-Kandasa.

Jeddah is a beautiful city located on the coast. It has a covered market which contains multi-storey buildings with traditional balconies. The Governor of the city was called Qa'im Maqam of Jeddah and we visited his office on the beach.

## Medina

The Saudi government hired two cars for us from the Bakhashab Pasha Company for Transporting Pilgrims. The driver of the main car was named 'Abdul-Rahman. He was a fat, heavy man, and the car was always weighed down on the side he was sitting. In the other car was Mubarak with our bags.

We left Jeddah after staying there for three days, and at midday headed for Medina along the coast. At sunset we stopped at a village on the Red Sea called Rabigh. There was a restaurant on the main road that served fried fish and fresh bread. We continued on our way after the sunset and evening prayers, arriving in Medina after midnight. We stayed in the Taysir Hotel, which had multiple floors, high ceilings and a staircase with large steps. It was located in the market area next to the Holy Mosque of the Prophet Muhammad.

The next day we visited the Prophet's Mosque. We performed two units of prayer and visited the tomb of the Prophet

Muhammad bin Abdullah (upon whom be Allah's peace and blessings). We paid our respects, and then my brother Khalid said a prayer. Touched by the sacredness of the place and the veneration of the Prophet, Khalid cried in reverence and we cried with him.

We also paid our respects at the tomb of the successor to the Prophet Muhammad, the Caliph Abu Bakr, and his successor, the Caliph 'Umar ibn al-Khattab. That afternoon we went to visit the cemetery of Al-Baqi', where the graves of the Prophet's Companions and his Followers are located. We paid our respects to all of them.

Before night fell in Medina, I saw a man carrying a number of lanterns that were lit and attached to a bar. He was carrying them on one of his shoulders, while in his other hand was another bar with a hook at the end of it. At certain places, the man stood and raised one lantern after another with the pole that had the hook at the end. He hung them on a metal wedge that was fixed to the highest part of the walls of the city. He continued doing that until a few moments later all the markets and streets leading to the Prophet's Mosque were lit up.

On the second day of our visit to Medina, we visited Mount Uhud (where the second battle of Islam took place), and paid our respects to the martyrs of Uhud. That evening we strolled through the markets of Medina.

## Mecca

On the morning of the third day, we left Medina to go to Mecca. We took the road that goes past Abu Hulaifa, the embarking point (*miqat*) for pilgrims from Medina. The road was unpaved and rocky. Nevertheless, the car drove over it easily and we arrived at the *miqat* of Dhi al-Hulaifa. There we entered a state of ritual consecration for our 'Umra (minor) pilgrimage, which involves praying and putting on the simple white sheets of the pilgrim. Then we circled the Ka'ba, the sacred black-draped square structure at the heart of the mosque, and performed the *sa'y* (the ritual walk in Mecca between the hills of Safah and Marwah). After performing the 'Umra, we came out of our ritual state of consecration. Then, when the time for standing on Mount 'Arafah approached, we entered a state of consecration for the Hajj (major) pilgrimage. We circled the Ka'ba once more, performed the *sa'y*, and then left for 'Arafah.

We entered Mecca at night, chanting '*Allahu Akbar!* (God is great!)' and declaring our profession of faith. We circled the Ka'ba and performed the *sa'y*. Some of us cut all our hair off, while others only clipped it. Then the vehicles took us to the Taysir Hotel in Jarwal, a neighbourhood in the city of Mecca, where we were to stay as guests of the Saudi government. From this moment we left our state of ritual consecration.

The next day I met the person in charge of meals at the hotel. He was an Egyptian named Mahmud, and he claimed that he had been a cook for King Farouq. He introduced me to a major general of the Saudi Interior Ministry, whose name was 'Abdul-Rahman. He was staying at the hotel during the Hajj season to oversee the security arrangements for the Hajj pilgrimage. I met him as he was about to leave for his work at the Hamidiyya Court. I asked him to take me with him to the Bushnaq bookshop, which was next to the Hamidiyya Court at the walkway for the *sa'y*, just before Mount Safah. I had seen that particular bookshop the previous night when I passed it as I was performing the *sa'y*. I asked him to recommend me to the person in charge of the bookshop as I wanted to spend some time browsing the books there. I didn't have any particular book in mind.

I sought the permission of my brother Khalid to go to Mecca after I introduced him to Major General 'Abdul-Rahman. Major General 'Abdul-Rahman introduced me to the owner of the Bushnaq bookshop, and it appeared to me that the two men knew each other. Mr Bushnaq gave me a chair to sit on while he took care of his duties in the shop.

The Bushnaq bookshop was located in the first section of the walkway, near Mount Safah. This first part of the walkway was cut off from the other parts by the only major road in Mecca. It was rocky and was the centre of a dry riverbed. That place is called Al-Harwala ('place of walking quickly'). Many pilgrims believed that people had to walk quickly there because of the cars passing through. The two other thirds of the walkway were a kind of covered market. On its sides were shops that went all the way to Mount Marwah. There was a metal fence between Safah and Marwah that separated the people who were coming from those who were going. The shopkeepers would smoke water pipes, and the smoke rose up and entered the courtyard of the Holy Mosque through the open doors on the side of the walkway.

The courtyard of the Mosque had a shrine for each of the four Imams: the Hanbali, Hanafi, Maliki and Shafi'i. Al-Shafi'i's shrine was on the building over the well of Zamzam. The other shrines were like umbrellas in the courtyard of the Mosque.

Around each shrine of the Imams people gathered to ask the assigned scholar about religious matters according to the precepts of their particular school.

The Gate of Ibrahim (Abraham) overlooked a group of rooms that were rented for the pilgrims. From these rooms came foul smells.

We stayed in Mecca for more than ten days, during which the door of the Ka'ba was opened. The male pilgrims poured in towards the door of the Ka'ba, where there was a rope hanging down from the roof of the building. The people held on to the rope, trying to lift themselves up to the door of the Ka'ba so that they could enter it. I held onto that rope until I got up above the heads of the others who were also holding onto it. Suddenly, one of them grabbed my *ghutra* which I had wrapped around my neck. He started pulling it down, thinking that it was the rope. I fell to the ground between the legs of those holding the rope. Praise be to Allah that I was not harmed by the feet that were stamping around me. I wrapped my *ghutra* around my waist and backed away from the men holding the rope. Then I ran as fast as I could and jumped onto the heads of the people holding the rope. I grabbed the rope, and then a person at the door of the Ka'ba grabbed my hand and pulled the rope towards him. I ended up inside the Ka'ba. It was dark inside, but a moment later I was able to see what was there. In the middle were two wooden pillars, and in the corner where the black stone was, a lamp was hanging. In the corner to the right of the door was a hole in the roof where light came in. It was here that the keepers of the Ka'ba went up onto the roof of the building. I prayed two units of prayer at each of the four corners.

On the eighth day of Zhu l-Hijja of the Islamic year 1374, which was the day of *tarwiya*, a Thursday, corresponding with 28 July 1955, we entered a ritual state of consecration and declared our intention to undertake the Hajj rites. We circled the Ka'ba, performed the *sa'y* and after that we went to Mina, where we stayed the night. The next day was the Day of 'Arafah, which fell on a Friday. We stood on Mount 'Arafah and made supplications to Allah. When the sun went down, everyone went on to Muzdalifah, and after that we went back to Mina. It was the Day of Sacrifice. We threw stones at the pillar at *jamarat al'aqabah* (one of the main principles of Hajj in remembrance of Ibrahim, Ismail and the Devil) and then I went with my brother Khalid and Mubarak to the place of the sacrifice. Khalid chose a fat bull, which was large enough to be a sacrifice for seven people, as we were seven in number.

After that, we cut our hair according to the requirement of the Hajj rites. The women only clipped some of their hair. We left the state of ritual consecration and put on our everyday clothes. Then we went to Mecca to perform the ritual of *ifadah*, the circling of the Ka'ba, and performed the *sa'y*.

My grandmother was not with us when we circled the Ka'ba and performed the *sa'y*, as she was ill. But it was necessary for her to circle the Ka'ba and perform the *sa'y* that evening to fulfil the requirements of the Hajj. My grandmother sat up on a bed, while two people lifted it up onto their heads. They circled the Ka'ba with her. For the *sa'y*, I sat her in a wheelchair and said to the owner of the chair, 'I will push her.'

The owner of the wheelchair agreed to this, and I began the *sa'y* with my grandmother. When we got to the final two units of *sa'y*, a group of boys saw me as new competition among the people doing that job there. I was wearing the clothing of the Hijaz region. The boys came and hit me until the wheelchair slipped out of my grasp. It began to roll quickly down the steep ground of Marwah, and my grandmother called out, 'Sultan! Sultan!'

I stood up against the separating fence in the walkway for the *sa'y*, and the boys beat me viciously. Then a group of African pilgrims who were holding onto each other pulled the boys away from me. However, these pilgrims also trampled on me. I screamed until people gathered around. They lifted me up from the ground, but I was not able to move in the crowd. I called out: 'Grandmother! Grandmother!' I finally reached her and started pushing her wheelchair again.

We spent the days of *tashriq*, the three days following the Day of Sacrifice, in Mina performing the throwing of stones (*jamrat*) ritual. Then we returned to Mecca, where we performed the final circuits of the Ka'ba. After that, we went to the airport at Jeddah, where we boarded planes for Dhahran airport.

We stayed in Dammam for two days, and then took two cars to Qatar via 'Ujair. In Qatar, we visited Shaikh 'Ali bin 'Abdullah Al Thani. From there we flew to Sharjah. The books I had left in Bahrain before the pilgrimage were freighted from Bahrain to Sharjah later.

Shaikh Sultan bin Saqr
al-Qasimi, former Ruler
of Sharjah (author's
uncle), 1942.

Sharjah Fort, 1950.

In front of Sharjah Fort: Shaikh Sultan bin Saqr al-Qasimi, former Ruler of Sharjah (*second from left*). To his right is Shaikh Saif bin Muhammad bin Mijlad, and to his left is a British guest. To the left of the guest is Minister Sayyid Ibrahim bin Muhammad al-Midfa', 1942.

Shaikh Muhammad bin Saqr al-Qasimi (author's father), Deputy Ruler of Sharjah, 1950.

Shaikh Rashid al-Maktoum, Deputy Ruler of Dubai, at the inauguration ceremony of Shaikh Saqr bin Sultan al-Qasimi (author's cousin) as the Ruler of Sharjah, 1951.

The first Qasimiyyah School football team, 1953–4. The author is in the first row, second from right.

The teacher Sharifa and her students in the second year girls' class at the Qasimiyyah School, 1954–5.

Ceremony held in the Qasimiyyah School (Ibn Kamil's house) to welcome the visiting delegation from Kuwait, 1955.

Cubs and Scouts of the Qasimiyyah School, 1955–6.

The author (on the right) as Scout Leader, 1957.

Football team at the Qasimiyyah School, 1955–6.

The author as a student at the Qasimiyyah School, 1956.

The author jumping through a ring of fire at the sports festival, 1956.

Sharjah Scouts' delegation at Kuwait airport; author first on the right, and in the middle is Mr Salim bin 'Abdullah al-Mahmoud, the representative of the Kuwait Ministry of Education.

Tehran, 1959: seated, from right to left: the author, Muhammad bin al-Shamisi, Taryam bin 'Umran, and Mr Shahini (owner of *Itla'at* newspaper in Iran); on the ground, right to left: 'Abdullah 'Umrani, Ya'qub bin Yusuf al-Dukhi.

Air base for the British warplanes, 1956.

Celebrations in Sharjah at the announcement of the unity agreement between Egypt, Syria and Iraq, 1963.

The parade ground in front of the guest house and the fort, crowded with citizens of Sharjah to greet Mr 'Abdul Khaliq Hassuna, Secretary-General of the League of Arab States, 1964.

Shaikh Khalid bin Muhammad al-Qasimi, author's brother and former Ruler of Sharjah, 1965.

The guest house, location of the *majlis* of Shaikh Saqr bin Sultan al-Qasimi, former Ruler of Sharjah, 1964.

The Trucial Oman Scouts accompanying Shaikh Khalid bin Muhammad al-Qasimi, the former Ruler of Sharjah, to the guest house in Sharjah, 1965.

The author in his first
year at the Faculty
of Agriculture, Cairo
University, 1965–66.

The author (*top right*) in
the Faculty of Arts, Cairo
University, 1969.

6

*The Tripartite Aggression against Egypt*

ON 29 OCTOBER 1956, BRITAIN, France and their spoilt child Israel launched an attack on Egypt. They struck the radio station known as Voice of the Arabs in Muqattam, and the station stopped broadcasting. After that, Voice of the Arabs was broadcast from Damascus. The people were outraged, but they had no power to do anything about it. They heaped curses on the aggressors, and called from their hearts for Egypt to be victorious. My mind was preoccupied. All I could think was: 'How can I make the aggressors lose, even if it is just by a whisker?'

## Reconnaissance

On 1 November 1956, I went out to the British base in Sharjah. My car was known to the officials at the base as I was one of the players on the football team of the British Ministry of Public Works at the British base in Sharjah. I was always contacting the players and informing them of the dates of matches. I would also take them to the games, as I was in charge of the team.

I made my way to the tank yard near the garage, where one of the players worked. His name was 'Abdul-Rahman Damuni. I had given him a lift home in my car many times after he finished work. We were good friends from playing football together.

When I got to the door of the workshop, I asked for 'Abdul-Rahman. He came out and I led him far away from the workshop, over to where I had parked my car. I took out some papers on which I had written the names of the players in English and the date of the next match. There was a strong westerly wind that day, and I deliberately let some of the papers fly out of my hands towards the direction of the tank yard, which was near the outer fence of the base.

I ran after the papers. The British guard standing at the door to the tank yard rushed in front of me and began reading them. He handed them to me and said, 'Good luck.'

One of the papers got stuck in the outer fence, which was made of barbed wire. I said to the British guard, 'I can't get it, as the wire is electrified.'

He responded, 'It is not electrified.'

I asked, 'Even at night?'

'Even at night,' he replied.

I went to pick up the piece of paper. I found out that the fence was made of three layers of barbed wire. Not even a cat could get through it.

On 2 November 1956, just after midday, I went to the British base to arrange a match with the team at the air-base. When I arrived at the gate of the base, there were some buildings at the side in which military aircraft were serviced. There was a car there, on the back of which in capital letters was written in English, 'FOLLOW ME'.

The car drove ahead of me, and I followed it along the runway towards the desert until it reached the ammunition store. The car stopped there and I stopped behind it. My eyes checked the ammunition store. The driver of the car got out, and angrily asked, 'Why are you following me?' I pointed to the sign on the back of his vehicle and said, 'You ordered me to follow you.'

He laughed and said, 'That sign is for the pilot of the aircraft, to guide him to the place where he will park the plane. Where were you going?' I replied, 'To meet the person in charge of your team, the team of the air-base, to organise a match with you.'

He said, 'Are you Sultan?'

'Yes,' I responded.

He said, 'Follow me.'

Half of the ammunition store was below the ground and the other half was raised a metre and a half above ground. In its walls were glass windows through which light could enter the store. There was no fence around the store.

That night, I walked the four kilometres from my house until I reached once again the ammunition store. I wanted to find out whether or not a guard was stationed there during the night.

The moon had gone down and the night was pitch dark. I was wearing dark clothes. Clumps of heliotrope and saltbush were growing all over the ground in the area between me and the building, which I estimated to be about three hundred metres away. I crawled on my belly until I got up close to the building. When I got there, I found that it was closely guarded and that a car was parked there. I came back, still crawling on my belly, to a place a little further away than before.

On the night of 3 November 1956, I went back to the British base. I intended to check how tight the security around the military aircraft was. I went exploring by walking down the main road at eight o'clock at night when the workers were coming and going after the change of shifts on the base. The security there consisted of two British soldiers, each carrying a rifle with fixed bayonet. The two soldiers would leave their posts to go to the bar in the hotel next to the airport to buy cans of beer. Then they would return and sit on the drums that were lined up to separate the military aircraft from the main road.

My presence there was not unusual, as some of the members of the football team to which I belonged worked in the hotel. It was the perfect place. It would be easy to carry out an operation against the aircraft from there.

In the afternoon of 4 November 1956, I went to the building housing the centre for wireless and telephone communications that was located between the British base and the city of Sharjah. This was a very important place as far as the international communications of the British base were concerned. Its importance also extended to controlling the air traffic passing overhead. I went there on the pretence that I would be meeting one of the players in the football team, an Indian engineer named Siddiqi.

I checked the place. On the outside there was no guard except at the main entrance to the building. Behind the building was a wooden gate which was shut and left unguarded. It had no walls surrounding it. When I got inside the building, I asked Siddiqi to take me around inside. I noticed that there were wires stretched across the back gate and an electric-powered device close to the gate. I was certain now that this would be an appropriate place.

On 5 November 1956, I headed to the desert to a region called Falaj. Here there was a pumping station that pumped water for the British base through pipes under the ground, except at one point where they had become exposed by the wind. I had seen that part many times when I went there to study. I noticed the exposed pipe, and made sure of where it was.

The following day, I left my house following the evening prayer and headed for the Sharjah district of Maraija. This was where the Gray Mackenzie Building was located, owned by the children of the late Shaikh Sultan bin Saqr al-Qasimi. It had once been rented to the British India Steam Navigation Company, but now it was being rented by the British Commander of the Trucial Oman Levies.

The car of the Saudi envoy in Buraimi (which the British Commander had been using after taking control of the town) was parked in front of the building. The British Commander had taken it for himself and deported the Saudi envoy and the Shaikhs of Buraimi to Saudi Arabia. The only guard there was an old man whose name was Ibn Mazhloum. He was sitting in front of the car. The place was perfect. After a full reconnaissance, I decided to get to work.

## The first operation

On 7 November 1956 I left our house after sunset and went to the car park; our car was in the garage there. There was an empty one-gallon oil can that I had used when I changed the oil in the car. I opened the plug at the bottom of the petrol tank in our car and filled the oil can from there, and then I returned to the house with the filled can.

I put on some black trousers, a dark brown pullover, and rubber shoes that I had worn in football matches and other sporting events. I left the house carrying the can of petrol and with a box of matches in my pocket. Two of my friends were sitting on the long bench in front of the gate to our house. One of them was Muhammad bin Sultan bin 'Abdullah, my classmate at school, and the other was Hamad bin 'Abdul-Rahman al-Manna'i, who was younger than us and was in a lower grade at school. I told them that I was taking some petrol to my car, which had stopped on the road between Dubai and Sharjah.

One of them said, 'We'll go with you.'

'There are women in the car,' I replied.

The other said, 'Then we'll take you there and you can come back to us after you take your family home.'

'Are you men?' I asked them.

'Yes, of course!' they replied.

'Are you afraid of death?'

'No!' they replied, in surprise.

Then I continued, 'Following the aggression against Egypt, every day we call for victory to Egypt and for defeat and humiliation for the aggressors, but we've done nothing. Now it is time for us to do something. You can help by either coming with me or just covering up for me.'

They both said, 'We will go with you.'

I went with them away from the town. They took turns carrying the can of petrol, until we were near the communications building. Then I said, 'Let's have a break for a moment.'

The building was one hundred metres from us. It was lit on the front side only, where the two armed guards sat. I then briefed them on my plan:

1. The ceiling of the building was covered with tar. If it was touched by a flame it would catch fire.

2. The back gate was large and made of wood. If petrol was poured onto it and set alight, the flames would reach the ceiling and the equipment inside the building as well.

3. Hamad would stay here. When he saw the flames, he would run quickly and wait for us by the palm-branch houses on the high ground.

Hamad al-Manna'i was shorter and heavier than the other two of us, so running was difficult for him. In contrast, I had come first in the 100-metre sprint and Muhammad bin Sultan had came second. In the 400-metre and 800-metre races, Muhammad bin Sultan had come first in both, while I was second. Therefore, Hamad al-Manna'i had to be given a head start so that he wouldn't lag behind.

The moon had begun to set, and when it went down I made my move. With me was Muhammad bin Sultan, who was carrying the can of petrol to the building. I told him to pour the petrol over the gate from the top, and then to move away. He poured the petrol over the gate until it dripped onto the cement step in front of it. The petrol could be heard falling. This frightened Muhammad bin Sultan, and so he threw down the petrol can and fled.

I rushed over and picked up the can, and found that there was still some petrol left in it. I poured the rest onto the gate and lit it. The step underneath me caught fire, where some petrol had collected as it had dripped from the gate. I jumped off the step and ran as quickly as my legs would take me. When I turned to look back, I saw bright flames licking the roof of the building, turning night into day.

The employees left the building and joined the guards, who were shouting out. Then they got into a car and headed towards us. I met up with Muhammad and then Hamad. We ran between the palm-branch huts from one hut to another. All the huts were unoccupied as the people only used them during their summer vacation. They were searching for us in the area around the huts, using light from the headlights of their cars, but we had already made it to the edge of the city and they could not find us.

## The second operation

The following morning, the talk of the town was of the fire that had occurred the previous night. At noon that day I went towards the car park, where there was a carpentry workshop owned by a man from Aden. His name was Salih al-'Adni. He left the doors of his workshop open and unguarded every day at midday. I went in and took a hacksaw which I could use to cut metal. I grabbed some extra blades as well. After the sunset prayer, Hamad al-Manna'i and Muhammad bin Sultan came to our house. From there we moved to the place outside the town where the wind had exposed the pipes that brought water to the base. Then I briefed them on my plans for that night.

We started cutting the metal pipe. Water spurted out of the pipe with force. We eventually cut right through the pipe. Nevertheless, we weren't able to separate one part of the pipe from the other, as it was heavy and buried in the ground. We left the water spurting out of it profusely.

In the town, nobody knew about that operation as it was far away in the desert.

## The third operation

On 9 November 1957, Hamad al-Manna'i came to me at midday to tell me that Muhammad bin Sultan would not be able to join us that night as he was busy.

'But the operation needs three people to carry it out,' I said.

Hamad al-Manna'i asked, 'What is the operation?'

'I don't know!' I replied.

Hamad al-Manna'i thought for a while, and then said, 'I know someone called 'Ali bin Khadim. He lives near our house, in Maraija.'

'Can we trust him?' I asked.

'Yes,' he replied.

'Then bring him with you after the sunset prayer.'

Hamad al-Manna'i and 'Ali bin Khadim came to our house after the sunset prayer carrying a can of petrol that I had bought at the petrol station. I poured half of it into my car so that it would be easier for us to carry. I also carried a wooden pole to which I had tied old pieces of cloth. I also had a box of matches in my pocket. Then we set off for Maraija.

Our intended destination was the home of the British

Commander of the Trucial Oman Levies. In Al-Ma'tam Lane, which was in front of our intended destination, I stopped with them to explain the plan, as follows:

- I would crawl under the car to explore the place.
- Hamad would bring me the can of petrol and take back the can when it had been emptied.
- 'Ali bin Khadim would get me the pole and then light it at one end.
- After the operation had been executed we would then leave by Al-Ma'tam Lane, and from there we would go via the *sabkha* on the way to Al-Jubail.

We went to the house of the British Commander. The back of his car was just in front of the open gate, facing south. A cement wall separated us from the car. I crawled under the car, and then saw the guard called Ibn Mazhloum sitting by the front wheel. Next to him was the boatman 'Abaduh, who transported people in a small boat (*'abra*) from Maraija to Layya. I could hear 'Abaduh asking to be excused as he wanted to go to the shop to buy some bread before it closed for the night, and Ibn Mazhloum saying to him, 'There is still time.'

I came out from under the car and asked for the can of petrol, emptied it out under the car below the petrol tank and gave the can back to Hamad. After that, 'Ali bin Khadim handed me the pole. The cloth which had been wrapped at one end of it was soaking in petrol. He lit it and I placed it under the car. The flames rose up. We then withdrew to Al-Ma'tam Lane from where we saw 'Abaduh running to the sea carrying a can to fetch water to put the fire out. However, the petrol tank of the Commander's car exploded, stopping 'Abaduh from getting close enough to the car to do anything.

The three of us fled to the *sabkha* towards Al-Jubail, and then returned to the site of the incident. People had gathered around the burnt-out frame of the car, we among them.

By 10 November 1957, the incident had become the talk of the town. It had also become the talk of our school. That day, the British Political Representative came to the school in his car from Dubai. British flags were fluttering on the car. The representative got out and entered the office of the headmaster of Qasimiyyah School, Mr Muhammad Dhiyab al-Musa. A few moments later, the representative came out, got back into his car and left the school.

I had been watching everything from the window of my classroom, and I kept watching. I saw the school janitor, 'Ubaid al-Taqi, leaving the office of the headmaster and coming toward my classroom. He knocked at the door and informed the teacher, 'The headmaster wants to see Sultan.'

My teacher then ordered me to go to the headmaster.

Before Mr Muhammad Dhiyab al-Musa said anything about the subject, he asked me to go to the schoolyard in front of his office and count the number of students at the school. I responded, 'I already know the number of students here. There are six hundred and seventeen.'

Mr Muhammad Dhiyab said, 'Do you want to prevent your brothers from getting an education, and your sisters in the Fatima al-Zahra School, too? I haven't spoken to and will not speak to any other student except you! Now return to your class!'

I was sure that my brothers and sisters would not be affected and I carried on with my struggle, disregarding his threats.

## *The fourth operation*

I returned to my class with even greater determination than before. The next operation would be major and would shake the world! Three British aircraft would be set on fire, aircraft that might have killed women and children in Port Said. I had collected a large number of rags from the piles of rubbish around the town to use in the operation. When the school day was over and we left the classroom, I whispered in the ear of Muhammad bin Sultan, 'Today is the day, after the sunset prayer!'

In the schoolyard, Hamad al-Manna'i came up to me and I told him, 'We meet today after the sunset prayer.'

Hamad asked, 'Should I bring 'Ali bin Khadim?'

'No,' I replied. 'This time Muhammad bin Sultan is coming. I have already talked to him about it.'

After the sunset prayer, Hamad al-Manna'i and Muhammad bin Sultan came. They carried a can of petrol that was open at the top. I had made two handles at the top to carry it with. There was a long rope in the can. I wrapped a large number of rags around the rope, and to one end I attached a stone. I was going to put it in the air inlet of the military aircraft and spread the rope wrapped in petrol-soaked rags out from it. Then I would light the end of it so that the fire would spread to the aircraft.

We arrived at the British base, and by the side of the road from Sharjah to the base we lay on our stomachs on the ground between heliotropes and saltbush so that we wouldn't be caught in the lights of passing cars or be seen by passers-by. We waited for a while until the workers from Sharjah were about to come to the base.

I told them that I would go to explore the place. I went quickly and came back. I informed them that there were two British soldiers standing in front of the door of the hotel drinking beer. Each of them had a rifle with a bayonet. They would spend some time there before returning to the aircraft enclosure to stand guard. Before they got back to the aircraft enclosure we would already have finished the operation.

Mohammad bin Sultan started to get afraid, and said, 'I'm not with you!'

'Why?' I asked.

He said, 'You talk about guns and bayonets, but you don't even have a knife!'

'I have faith, which is stronger than guns and bayonets,' I replied.

Then Hamad al-Manna'i intervened, saying, 'Let him go back. I am still with you!'

'Go quickly, and don't stop,' I told him. 'They will be looking for us in cars, just as they did at the wireless transmission building.'

We waited for a while until Muhammad bin Sultan reached the city of Sharjah. Then I said to Hamad al-Manna'i, 'Let's go! We are very late now because of him!' We carried the can of petrol and the long rope to the aircraft enclosure. The place was quiet except for the sound of crickets chirping in the night. They had gathered particularly around that spot.

I asked Hamad, 'Do you hear that?'

'What?'

'The sound of the crickets. If you see anything, make a sound like the crickets to warn me.'

We were now under the lamp post which shone light onto three military aircraft. There was a dark spot under the lamp post.

We hid in the dark spot among the drums that had been arranged as a fence between the aircraft enclosure and the main road, and in front of us was the middle plane.

I got out the end of the rope which was attached to the stone, and whispered to Hamad, 'When I am under the plane, throw the rock to me along with a part of the rope.'

I crawled to the middle plane, which was very close to where we were. That type of aircraft was low, and very close to the ground. It cast a dark shadow. Suddenly I heard a voice: 'Chirp, chirp, chirp!'

I turned to Hamad, and he pointed to the south. I turned around and saw two pairs of legs approaching. I could only see the soldiers from the knees down. I turned my thin body to a wheel of the plane in order to blend in with my dark clothing.

The two soldiers moved into the space between the first and the middle aircraft. One of them said to the other, 'Give us a cigarette.'

The other said, 'Not here. Let's move away from the planes a bit.'

The soldiers moved a few metres away. Each of them tried to light the cigarette, but the wind kept blowing the flame out. They came closer to each other to light the cigarette. I had by that time crawled to the area where the drums were, and had begun crawling in the dark for some distance. Then I got up to find Hamad waiting for me.

'Where is your plan now?!' he said.

I replied, 'The problem was only caused by a few minutes' delay. Muhammad bin Sultan made us late when we had that argument with him.' Then I asked Hamad, 'Where is the can of petrol?'

'I left it there between the drums, near the middle plane,' he replied.

I said, 'The two soldiers are always sitting on those drums in that dark spot where you left it. Let's wait for a moment until they get thirsty and head to the hotel for a drink.'

We returned to the aircraft enclosure to complete the operation. We saw a number of soldiers and military vehicles coming to the place where we had left the can of petrol. I said to Hamad, 'The British have found the can of petrol. Let's get out of here.'

He replied, 'To the city?!'

'No,' I said, 'to the desert! Along the fence of the base.'

The military vehicles began patrolling with lights around the place where we were located, and then headed for the city. We hurried to the desert, heading north so that we could enter the city from the north, as we had left from the southern side.

## Dawn prayer

I arrived at my house just before dawn. I entered the big room where we used to sleep. That room was called the *makhzan* (large bedroom), and most of my family slept there.

My father was sleeping on a bed on one side of the room. My

mother was asleep with her small children, my brother 'Abdullah and my sister Na'ima, who were sleeping on mattresses on the ground. The other bed was in the other corner of the *makhzan*. I sneaked over to the other bed and lay down on it. But I couldn't sleep. I stayed awake until I heard my mother call my father when he got up to perform the dawn prayer. She said, 'Muhammad . . . Muhammad . . .'

My father replied, 'Yes?'

My mother said, 'Deal with this child. For a number of days he has been coming back at dawn!'

'I am too embarrassed to talk to him,' my father replied.

My mother asked, 'How can you be embarrassed with your own son?!'

My father left his bed and went to the bathroom to perform his ablutions; this was called the *qati'a* ('divide'). When he had finished his ablutions, he stood at the door that separated the *makhzan* from the bathroom and called out to me, 'Sultan . . . Sultan . . .'

'Yes?' I answered.

My father said, 'Do your ablutions. Let's go to the mosque.'

I got up quickly, and before I had even reached the door to the bathroom area my father's body was blocking it. I tried to pass through the gap. My father grabbed my shoulders with both his hands and made me face him. He stared at me as if his eyes were asking, 'Are you the one who did these things?'

I nodded my head as if to reply, 'Yes . . . It was me.'

My father held me to his chest and kissed me. My mother heard the sound of the kiss and said, 'You are a strange man. Rather than chastising the boy, you kiss him for what he did!'

My father replied, 'Maryam, this boy did something that I couldn't do.'

As he stared at my face, the Muezzin gave the call to the morning prayer . . .

*Allahu Akbar, Allahu Akbar* (God is great, God is great).

# 7

*Events in Sharjah*

T<small>HE CITY OF SHARJAH WAS</small> quiet. The labourers and employees would leave early in the morning from their houses in the city to their jobs at the airport or at the British base to the south of Sharjah. After that the students would come out of their houses. The boys would go to the Qasimiyyah School, which was located between the city of Sharjah and the airport, and the girls would go to their school in the city centre.

Many events took place in the city in the period 1958–59. I will relate some of these.

### Exile of the teachers

At the end of the school year 1956–57, Mr Hashim 'Imara, the Palestinian headmaster of the Dubai School, was exiled from Dubai at the behest of the British staff at the Kuwait Office in Dubai, where the Kuwaiti Education Mission was located. Mr Faiz Abu Na'aj, a Palestinian teacher from the Qasimiyyah School in Sharjah, had also been exiled, both of them for agitating the students against the British. All attempts by Shaikh Saqr bin Sultan al-Qasimi (on the grounds that he was the private teacher to his son) to keep him had been fruitless. The greatest damage was done to the Qasimiyyah School when the British decided to prevent Mr Muhammad Dhiyab al-Musa, the headmaster of the school, from returning to Sharjah. He was also accused of agitating the students against the British and especially because of what had happened in Sharjah. When the school opened for the 1957–58 school year, there was no headmaster. So the Kuwait Office in Dubai requested that one of the teachers be appointed as deputy headmaster until a new headmaster arrived.

Since Mr Muhammad Dhiyab al-Musa had come to teach at the Qasimiyyah School he had added school activities every year as well as raising the standard of education. His last activity was the annual sports festival that was held every April. It was attended by Shaikhs from the different emirates and a large group of people from Dubai, Sharjah and ʿAjman. There was also a performance of the well-known play *Masked Honour*, which was written by the Palestinian poet Mahmud Ghonaim. I played the main role which was that of Jabir ʿAtharat al-Kiram, which literally means 'Saviour of the Nobles' Mistakes'. A number of Shaikhs from the different emirates attended, along with a large number of people who had purchased tickets on the days of the Eid holiday that preceded the performance of the play. An estimated 32,000 rupees was collected, most of which had come from donations by the Shaikhs of the emirates. The donation made by Shaikh Rashid bin Saʿid al-Maktoum, the Ruler of Dubai, was particularly generous. The money that was collected was to go to the building of extra classrooms for the Qasimiyyah School in Sharjah.

## Middle school exams in Kuwait

Before the end of the 1957–58 school year, when we were in the fourth grade of the middle school, was the time of the middle school certificate examinations for the Qasimiyyah School in Sharjah. This was the first examination of its kind, and students were required to travel to Kuwait to take it.

The Department of Education in Kuwait hired a special plane from Gulf Air to take us to Kuwait via Bahrain. We were thirteen students in total. The supervisor in charge of the trip was Mr Jasim bin Saif al-Midfa', who was assisted by Sidqi Dhiyab al-Musa, the brother of Mr Muhammad Dhiyab al-Musa.

When we arrived at Kuwait airport, the official examining our passports burst out laughing. He talked to a second employee, then a third, and then a fourth. One of the officials came to return our passports after stamping them with an entry stamp while laughing. He said, 'All born on the same day?'

We couldn't answer, as we didn't understand what he meant! We looked at our passports and found that Mr Gharib 'Abdul-Salihin from the Egyptian Mission, who had written our names in the passports, had written the date of birth for all of us as 1/1/1942, thus making us objects of ridicule. We stayed in Kuwait at house number 12 of the houses at the Shuwaiykh Secondary School, and the middle school examination went smoothly.

After that, the Education Department took us in a bus to Ahmadi to see the city and the oil installations there. We had a day to relax before we left Kuwait for Sharjah. I hired a car to take me to the Abu Hulaifa School outside Kuwait City, where I visited my former headmaster Mr Muhammad Dhiyab al-Musa, who was now a teacher there. I asked him, 'What made you choose me of all people to give a warning to during the events of 1956?' Mr Muhammad Dhiyab al-Musa replied, 'The teachers who were teaching you had informed me that Sultan al-Qasimi was passing through a particular mental state, and he was no longer the same person he had been. They said that you were an exemplary student, to the extent that you would follow the teacher with your eyes wherever he went, even when he went to the back of the class. But on that day, you were absent-minded.'

We left Kuwait on the hired Gulf Air plane to return to Sharjah. The plane had to be refuelled in Bahrain while we waited in transit. As soon as our plane arrived in Bahrain, a health officer entered the plane and asked for our health cards. It became apparent that the person in charge of our trip had left them in Kuwait.

He said, 'You must be given vaccinations.'

I went to him and said, 'We have no business here in Bahrain.'

'You must have your health cards with you,' he replied.

Opening up my passport, I said, 'Look. Here is the entry stamp for Kuwait and this is the exit stamp for Kuwait. Therefore, how would they have let us into Kuwait?'

He replied, 'This is of no concern to me.'

I said as I rolled up one of my sleeves, 'Look . . . The vaccination wound is still festering!'

He replied, 'This is a wound on your arm!'

I said to all of the students, 'Show him your arms.'

They showed him their arms, and he said, 'Even so . . . You must be vaccinated.'

'By God . . .' I said, 'this is not going to happen!'

He replied, 'By God . . . The plane is not going anywhere!'

We sat for a quarter of an hour, and all the students begged me to agree to the vaccination. They said, 'It is just a small wound made with a scalpel.' The health officer asked all of us to get out of the plane and to go to the airport building. We waited until the health officer came.

'Where is the doctor who will be giving us the vaccinations?' I asked him.

'It's me,' he replied.

I said in astonishment, 'You?!'

'Am I not good enough for you? Do I have to be a foreigner to be good enough for you?'

'God forbid. But you could have given the vaccination before when our arms were exposed.'

'I did not have the vaccine in the aeroplane. The vaccine is here in the fridge.'

The doctor administered the vaccinations until all the students had been vaccinated. Only I remained alone with him.

I said, 'I have sworn an oath . . . I'll die if I don't stand by it, and I don't think you want me to die.'

'No, I don't,' he said.

I said, 'Give me the scalpel and I will cut my arm and do the vaccination under your supervision.'

'Agreed,' he replied.

And that's how it went.

## *Weapons failure*

At the end of 1958 there were a lot of stray dogs in the city of Sharjah. Shaikh Saqr bin Sultan al-Qasimi, the Ruler of Sharjah, ordered that they be disposed of.

One evening I heard shooting in the courtyard of the fort, so I went outside our house to find out what was going on. I came across a soldier who had killed a dog. He pointed his rifle at another dog, which sought my protection. But the bullet hit the dog at the base of its spine, and it fell to the ground. It began to drag the rear of its body around, which had become paralysed.

I scolded the soldier until he moved away, and I carried the dog to our house. I treated her and made a house for her out of wood. I took care of her by feeding, cleaning and giving her water until her wound healed. Every time I tried to leave the dog she followed me, dragging the rear part of her body around. I tried to take her back to her house, but she would start playing with me, looking at me as if she was asking me to stay with her.

Whenever I came home from school, the first thing I did was to make sure she was alright. One day I found her wet and trembling! Who had washed her?! And who had put that rope around her neck?!

I discovered a trail which showed that she had dragged her wet body from the western gate. I followed the trail and found that it went from the side of the market located on the beach. I asked the shopkeepers there if they had seen a paralysed dog pass by. They replied that a person had dragged a dog by a rope around its neck and thrown it into the sea. The person had tried to drown the dog, but it swam away and didn't come near the shore. When I finally returned to the house I found her dead.

In another place, young men had gathered to watch a soldier who was pointing his rifle at another dog that was sniffing through the rubbish. There was a person there who was wearing clothing that was just like ours, and he was hiding among us. When someone spoke to him, he pointed to his ears to indicate that he couldn't hear, and to his mouth as if to indicate that he couldn't speak either. The only sounds he uttered were, '*Hop . . . Ay . . . Hop.*'

The soldier aimed his rifle towards the dog, and everyone waited for him to fire. The sound of the rifle came: 'Click.'

The *Hop . . . Ay . . . Hop* man said: 'It failed.'

It was apparent then that he was an imposter. The young men of the town turned to him and grabbed him, but he slipped from their grasp and fled from the town.

It turned out later that he was a spy for the British.

There was a man named Sayyid 'Abdullah, who had given himself the title 'Leader of the Baluchis'. He lived in Sharjah. Sayyid 'Abdullah was among the group of Baluchis who had rebelled against Reza Shah in Iran twenty years before. He had fled with many other people and settled in Sharjah, taking up citizenship there. At that time he was carrying a passport issued in Sharjah. He was one of the men of Shaikh Saqr bin Sultan al-Qasimi, the Ruler of Sharjah. The Shaikh had paid him over the years a total of two hundred rupees a month.

On 9 December 1958, a dispute erupted in Sharjah between a Baluchi man and his wife. The Baluchi man was brought before Shaikh Saqr, who said that the issue needed to be brought before

Shaikh Saif al-Midfa', who was the judge in Sharjah. Shaikh Saif was asked to settle the dispute between the man and his wife.

When Sayyid 'Abdullah heard of this he refused to allow the Baluchi man to take his case to Shaikh Saif. He went to meet Shaikh Saqr in person on the evening of 11 December in the main *majlis*. Sayyid 'Abdullah said to Shaikh Saqr that the Baluchi people were under his authority, and that it was his duty to mediate in their disputes. Shaikh Saqr had grown weary of the protests of Sayyid 'Abdullah, and asked him to be quiet. He asked him to leave the *majlis*. Sayyid 'Abdullah then pulled out a pistol and pointed it at Shaikh Saqr. An Egyptian teacher named Muhammad 'Abul-Ma'ati was sitting in the *majlis*. He struck Sayyid 'Abdullah from behind and took away his gun. At the same time, Shaikh Saqr took a rifle from one of his men, aimed it at Sayyid Abdullah and pulled the trigger. But the weapon didn't fire. He tried to fire the rifle again, but the bullet didn't leave the rifle. Then Shaikh Saqr's guards grabbed Sayyid 'Abdullah. After beating him up, they marched him off to jail.

Shaikh Saqr threatened to deliver Sayyid 'Abdullah to the Iranian authorities, as he was wanted by them. Then the leader of all Baluchis on the Omani Batinah coast, Mirza Berkut, came to take Sayyid 'Abdullah with him to Oman. Mirza Berkut pledged that Sayyid 'Abdullah would not return to Sharjah.

At the end of December 1958 a fire broke out in a palm-branch tent in the Baluchi Quarter, and the lady who owned the tent was burnt to death. The lady's husband was accused of setting fire to the tent.

The Baluchi man was arrested and brought before the judge.

He was sentenced to death by firing squad but Sayyid 'Abdullah, the self-styled leader of the Baluchi people in Sharjah, was no longer in Sharjah, and so there was no one to defend the man. They led him outside the city to a place near the Rolla tree, where the Eid festivities and celebrations were normally held, to carry out the execution.

I was at that time leaving our house to see the execution, as were the other people, who were making their way quickly towards the Rolla tree.

At the door of our house, the Baluchi woman who used to sweep our house was standing there, frozen. Tears were pouring from her eyes. She asked, 'Where are you going?'

I replied, 'To see the man's execution.'

'Don't go!' she said.

I asked, 'Why not?'

'This is injustice!'

'How?!' I asked.

She said, 'I am the neighbour of the woman who was burnt. Our tents don't have walls or fences, and her husband wasn't home. She was cooking, and the tent caught fire. Then she got burnt.'

'Do you have any witnesses to this?' I asked.

'Yes . . . All the people in the area witnessed it.'

I ran quickly, even though she was still talking, until I arrived at the Rolla tree. I found the man with his hands and legs bound. The people of Sharjah were standing in lines to watch the execution. There was a man there called Salim al-Batini, an expert executioner and cutter of hands. He was loading his gun in preparation for the execution.

147

I stood in front of him and asked him not to shoot. I informed him, 'This man is innocent . . . I have witnesses to prove it!'

I grabbed the barrel of the gun, which now became pointed at my chest!

Salim al-Batini said, 'Grab him . . . The gun is loaded.'

They grabbed me and I lost my grip on the barrel of the rifle.

Salim al-Batini aimed the rifle toward the Baluchi man . . . but it didn't fire!!

I screamed, 'Enough!! Enough!!'

I tried to free myself from the guards, but I wasn't able to. Then Salim al-Batini aimed his gun again and fired. The Baluchi man fell down. I ran to him, thinking that I could take him to hospital. When I lifted his head, I saw that he had passed away. His eyes were still open and looking at me, as if saying, 'Thank you.'

## Separation from my parents

In 1957, Shaikh Muhammad bin 'Ali Al Thani, son of the Ruler of Qatar, married my sister Na'ima. Because of her young age, my mother moved with her to Qatar. Our house had no life. A year had gone by since the marriage and I went to Qatar in June 1958 to see my mother and sister, who now had a baby boy named 'Abdullah.

I stayed in Qatar for a month. During that time, I visited the cities, villages and beaches of Qatar. I saw the development that had taken place since my first visit three years earlier. One day, I visited the Doha harbour, where there were wooden ships that brought goods from all the ports in the Gulf region, India,

Pakistan and East Africa. On one side of the port I saw a number of trucks unloading cargoes of rocks into the sea. When I asked about this, I was told that it was the beginnings of the port of Doha that was being built.

There are no mountains in Qatar. So where did those lorries carrying rocks come from? I followed the trucks in my car and found them carrying them from a quarry several kilometres to the south of Doha. Those milky coloured rocks were covered in desert sand.

At the beginning of July 1958, I decided to return by plane to Sharjah. On its way the plane landed at Abu Dhabi airport, which had been constructed a few months earlier. It consisted of a reclaimed salt flat which was made into a runway, and had a temporary building for passengers. At the end of the runway, the plane left the levelled ground and one of its wheels sank in the soft marsh until its wing touched the ground. A car sped from the passenger terminal, and after they found out what had happened a four-wheel-drive vehicle arrived and the driver got out. His name was Mashallah, and he was from Sharjah. He tied a metal cable to the axle of the plane after digging around the wheel. Then he dragged out the plane that had refused to move.

The management of Abu Dhabi airport decided to request another plane from Bahrain to take us to Sharjah. We got into the car with Mashallah. There were only two of us going to Sharjah: Ibrahim bin Nassar and myself. He took us to a restaurant built of palm branches on the beach in Abu Dhabi, where we ate lunch. Then he took us on a trip around important sites in Abu Dhabi, such as the Fort. The fort was white and had towers from which you could see areas outside the town, and which were separated from the town by soft, white sand. On the beach there were some buildings that had been erected for the companies operating in Abu Dhabi.

I asked Mashallah, 'Is the plane coming from Bahrain just for me and Ibrahim?'

Mashallah said, 'The plane is coming to carry a large consignment of gold that was on your plane. That is why the wheels of the plane sank in the *sabkha*.'

That consignment of gold was transported from Bahrain to Sharjah, and from there it was to be smuggled to India.

One evening before the school year began, my father slipped in the bathroom and broke his leg in the middle of his thigh. Because I was the closest when he called out, I put him in the car and took him to the Al-Maktoum Hospital in Dubai.

His children and other relatives crowded the hospital to visit him and to find out if he was alright. My brother Khalid discussed my father's treatment with the doctors. They came to the conclusion that he should be transferred to Qatar for treatment, and so my brother Khalid and I flew to Qatar. I stayed only a short time and then returned to Sharjah to continue my studies.

At the hospital in Qatar, my father's broken bone could not be put in a cast. So it was decided that he should be taken to the Barbir Hospital in Beirut, to have an operation to insert a metal rod into the bone cavity. The operation was completed successfully at the beginning of 1959, and it was only a month before my father was able to walk again on both legs.

But at dawn on 4 February 1959, while still in Beirut, my father suffered a stroke. A telegram arrived for Shaikh Saqr bin

Sultan al-Qasimi, the Ruler of Sharjah, telling him what had happened. He travelled to Beirut to get a first-hand report on the health of his uncle.

A representative of the Government of Qatar in Lebanon immediately asked the British Embassy to send a prominent surgeon from London to carry out an urgent operation. At half past two on the afternoon on 5 February 1959, a BOAC plane arrived in Beirut. On board was the British surgeon Murray Falconer, who was from Guy's Hospital. He had carried out a similar operation a year earlier on Hamid Farangieh. The doctor was accompanied by his assistant, Dr Hamilton.

Upon the arrival of Mr Falconer, my father's operation was carried out and he regained consciousness. However, the stroke had affected one of his hands and one of his legs. He returned to Sharjah at the beginning of March 1959, where he remained confined to his bed.

## Fire in Sharjah

One afternoon in March 1959, a strong wind from the south (the *suhaili*) blew up a dust storm. Meanwhile, a fire started and the wind spread the flames into the neighbourhood of the Baluchis, who were opposed to the Shah of Iran. Also there were the followers of Sayyid 'Abdullah, who had been exiled from Sharjah to Muscat, in Oman, several months earlier.

The fire consumed the houses, one by one, and the glowing palm cinders flew ahead of the fire to other houses far away, which were thatched with palm leaves. The Baluchi neighbourhood and other adjacent neighbourhoods were built entirely from palm branches. Consequently, the fire spread throughout the entire area, destroying everything in its path and leaving the families who lived there homeless.

Two days after the fire, a number of Iranian aircraft arrived at Sharjah airport. They were loaded with tents and blankets, and Shaikh Saqr bin Sultan al-Qasimi was given 100,000 rupees from the Iranian government to assist those affected by the fire.

## Military aircraft crash in Sharjah

On the morning of 10 March 1959, we were in our classroom when suddenly the sound of an explosion shook the walls of the classroom. The students went outside to investigate what had happened. They found that a British warplane of the Hunter type had crashed at Sharjah airport, which was only a few hundred metres away from the school.

This was not the only military plane to crash at Sharjah airport. After that, another British military plane of the Canberra type crashed, on 5 July 1959. I had nothing to do with those two incidents.

# 8

*A Trip to Iran*

CLOSE TO OUR HOUSE THERE lived an Iranian doctor called Ja'far, who had a medical clinic in Sharjah in the year 1958. Dr Ja'far received a visit from his younger brother, who had come from Iran, and Dr Ja'far introduced me to him. After we had met a few times, Dr Ja'far's brother invited me to accompany him to visit his country.

I invited my friends Taryam bin 'Umran bin Taryam, his brother 'Abdullah bin 'Umran bin Taryam, Muhammad bin Hamad al-Shamsi and Ya'qub bin Yusuf al-Dukhi, and they agreed to join me on the trip.

I asked my bedridden father to write a letter to Major General Rahmani, the Iranian government official responsible for my father during his treatment in Tehran a few years earlier, asking him to take care of us.

Dr Ja'far wrote the letter in Persian, and my father stamped his seal on it. We rented a motor boat called *Sons of Zamzam* to take us from Sharjah to Linga, on the coast of Iran.

## *The sea voyage to Linga*

In the final days of July 1959, after the sunset prayer, all of us, including Dr Ja'far's brother, embarked on the boat. The boat's captain was a young man named 'Abaduh and assisting him in navigating was an older man called Khalfan. There was nobody else on the boat.

As the boat ploughed on, a heated debate grew between Taryam bin 'Umran, who was a fanatical supporter of Jamal Abdel Nasser, and Dr Ja'far's brother, who was likewise fanatical in his love for the Shah of Iran. I translated the argument into Persian as best I could, but left out much of what was said. I translated some of the words incorrectly, causing resentment between the two. One of them was holding my left hand and the other was holding my right. I wasn't able to translate words that were not in my Persian vocabulary, such as 'non-aligned countries' and other such phrases . . .

I extricated myself from the argument and went to the bows of the boat, where Captain 'Abaduh was sitting. He began to tell me of the horrors of the sea. As he was talking, a giant oil tanker passed close by, heading for the world's oil markets. 'Abaduh leapt over to the engine room and said to me, 'Push the tiller to the left,' while putting the engine to full speed. Everyone was asleep by now, including Khalfan, who was responsible for steering the boat. Our boat was very small compared to the giant oil tanker. When our boat passed by the bow of the tanker, our own bow was lifted up and the stern appeared to be submerged in the sea. The noise from the engines of the oil tanker changed and 'Abaduh said, 'He has seen us!!! He is stopping the oil tanker.'

I asked, 'In this darkness?'

He replied, 'He sees the lantern hanging on our mast.'

Our boat was moving through the water as fast as it could and left the oil tanker in its wake, which by now had stopped moving. Then our ship steered towards the left of the oil tanker, and Captain 'Abaduh stopped the boat.

I asked him, 'Why did you stop?'

He replied, 'To adjust our course.'

'Abaduh stood up and got out a large compass. He started turning it in the light of the lantern, which he had taken down from the mast. He was mumbling words to himself until he seemed to have reached a conclusion. Then he said, 'All right! I have found the course.'

I asked 'Abaduh, 'Wouldn't it have been better to let the tanker go and continue on our way after that?'

'If we had done that, we would have been finished!'

'Why's that?' I asked.

He replied, 'Behind the oil tanker at this speed, the high waves that it makes would have overturned our boat and sent it to the bottom of the sea.'

Our boat continued on its way until 'Abaduh stopped it and asked me to drop anchor.

'But we are in the middle of the sea!' I exclaimed.

He said, 'We are right in front of Linga.'

I dropped anchor, and waited to see what Linga looked like.

The sound of the call to prayer came from afar . . . *Allahu Akbar!*

I heard the continual crowing of roosters . . . and the faint sound of voices . . .

157

The buildings on the coast, which stretched north and south, turned golden in colour as the dawn broke behind us, and when the sun appeared and climbed up into the sky the houses glowed bright white, showing beautiful traditional embellishments built by my ancestors who had ruled the Persian coast centuries ago, when most of the inhabitants were Arabs.

When we got out onto the beach, we were received by Ahmad bin 'Abdullah al-Sa'di, who had also received a letter of recommendation from my father. We went to the guest house which was owned by the family of Reis al-Sa'di (a great merchant on that coast). There were no hotels in Linga in those days but Reis al-Sa'di had extensive connections and many visitors. He was the agent for many commercial ships.

## The road to Shiraz

The family of Reis al-Sa'di were generous, hosting us for several days when the flight from Linga to Shiraz, which we were meant to have taken there, was cancelled. We were forced to rent a car to take us to Shiraz instead.

We got a letter from the Governor of Linga after visiting his office. The letter contained a recommendation for us so that we could pass easily through all the checkpoints set up on the way to stop smugglers.

We got into the car, the front of which was covered and the back open. Dr Ja'far's brother filled it with two large boxes of smuggled goods for which customs had not been paid in Linga and bags of our clothes; then he covered them with carpets and rugs. The owner of the car was also the driver. His name was Marzuq and he worked as the assistant mechanic to Yusuf al-Dukhi, the father of our colleague Ya'qub bin Yusuf al-Dukhi, in the auto repair shop in Sharjah.

We left Linga in the afternoon and headed west, away from the coast and towards the mountains. After we had passed the villages of Ras Bustana and Shinas in the distance, we found ourselves on a plain in which trees and bushes were growing. Suddenly, soldiers were blocking the way of the car, among them a thin man who was wearing military shirt and trousers. It appeared from the way he was giving orders that he was an officer. He came from between the trees and ordered that we be inspected. At this point, Dr Ja'far's brother said, 'We have a letter from the Governor of Linga that states we are not to be inspected.'

The officer replied, 'Orders from the Governor of Linga apply only in Linga, and not here.'

The officer pulled up the carpet we had been sitting on and found our bags. He opened one of them and started rummaging through it and inspecting it with one of his dirty hands. With the other hand he held the letter from the Governor of Linga.

Dr Ja'far's brother said, 'I am an officer from the Interior Ministry in Shiraz.'

'You don't look like an officer,' the officer said. 'Give me a pen.'

Dr Ja'far's brother gave him a pen and said, 'Don't dirty my pen.'

The officer, who was getting angry now, called out, 'Soldiers!!'

Then the soldiers came out from between the trees and surrounded the car, and the officer walked over to a nearby tent.

An old man, who had asked us to give him a lift to his village while we were on our way to Shiraz, said, 'The officer has seen the large box under the carpet.'

The officer came back quickly after putting on his military jacket and said to us, 'I am taking you to Linga.' When he was about to go to the car, I grabbed him and patted his chest. Immediately, one of his soldiers brought his hand down like a club onto my hand. He pointed the bayonet of his rifle at my side, rebuking me and hurling insults: 'You dare to put your hand on the chest of the officer?!'

I raised both my hands in surrender. Dr Ja'far's brother immediately jumped out of the car, grabbed the officer and walked away with him by his side. We thought a fight would break out between them, but Dr Ja'far's brother opened the bag he was carrying, took out some papers and showed them to the officer. The officer came back in great haste, stamped his foot on the ground in front of me, raised his hand and gave a salute. Then he bowed and said repeatedly, 'I am sorry, Shaikh. I truly apologise for my conduct.'

He then turned to his soldiers and called for them to line up. He called out a second time and shouted an order for them to salute.

When the soldiers raised their guns to salute, and the officer raised his hand and saluted, I got into the back of the car. Taryam bin 'Umran said, 'Don't get in the back . . . Sit next to the driver Marzuq.' I said, 'It's really hot in the front seat!' Taryam bin 'Umran replied, 'Sit for a while . . . as befits a person of high status. After the car has moved away then you can get into the back seat.'

I sat next to the driver Marzuq. My head and my right hand were outside the car waving a salute to the officer, who disappeared into the dust thrown up by the wheels of the car.

The car was crossing the mountain chain, swaying on the rough road. When darkness descended, nothing was left in the world except for our car and the beam of the headlights that extended a few metres in front of us.

The car stopped suddenly after passing a flat plain and Marzuq called out, 'Everybody out! We have arrived in Maghuh, my home country!'

People got out and went to the toilet, while others spread blankets on the ground. Marzuq disappeared for a moment and returned with food and water. After we had finished eating our dinner, I asked Marzuq to take me to see the fort of Shaikh Sultan bin Ahmad al-Marzuqi, the Shaikh of Maghuh. The house of Shaikh Sultan al-Marzuqi was very large. It comprised two storeys and a number of windows which from the top floor overlooked the grounds, in which there were no houses. The entrance opened into a roofed passageway which had a number of *majlises* on each side.

We got back into the car, and as soon as it moved off every one of us fell into a deep sleep due to our complete exhaustion.

I woke up to the sound of Marzuq calling out, 'This is the town of Kukhird.' I opened my eyes to see walls made of mud brick to right and left. The car went through the streets of the town and we woke up again to the sound of Marzuq calling, 'Everybody out! We have arrived at the town of Bastak . . . You will be sleeping here.'

We spread the rugs on the ground, and we couldn't see anything around us at all. When the light of the sun struck me in the morning, I woke up and had a look around.

There was a shop . . . and in front of it was a man baking bread.

There was a building, partially dilapidated, with a face, round like the moon, looking over the balcony from the top floor . . . in a house which showed signs of wealth.

We paid the owner of the shop for our breakfast, which consisted of bread and fried eggs. But he held his open hand out in front of us.

We asked, 'What?'

He replied, 'Pay up! The fee for you sleeping on the side of the road! It's not for me . . . It's the fee for the local council.'

We got into our car and took off . . . The round face was still looking down from the balcony. I waved my hand to say good-bye, and she waved back to me.

The sun was high in the sky when we passed through a town called Harmud, which was about two hundred metres from the road and located in a ravine. Our car stopped near a shop on the road, where we bought some bread and yoghurt. The shop was as hot as an oven. I started eating the bread dipped in the yoghurt under the burning sun. Then a young man arrived from the town of Harmud. He knew me, so he invited me to his house. I politely declined the invitation and he ran back to the town. Then he came back again with a live billy goat and gave it to me. I declined his gift and thanked him for his generosity. We drove on towards the town of Lar, leaving the young man from Harmud still holding the billy goat in his arms.

That afternoon we arrived at a car park in the town of Lar. We asked for the house of the relatives of Reis al-Sa'di, and we were directed to it. Their relative Yusuf al-Baluki was waiting for us. After greeting us, he said, 'The telegram that reached me from Linga said that you would arrive at noon today. You are late.'

Yusuf al-Baluki took us to the guest house of Reis al-Sa'di. The *majlis* was cool from the air conditioner, which blew all day. There were cotton cushions around the walls as well as mattresses to sit on. We sat on the mattresses and reclined on the cushions. We felt sleepy, so we lay down on the mattresses. I stretched out my legs and kicked some plates that were arranged near me. I sat up to see that the floor of the *majlis* was spread with different kinds of food, with meat, sweets and fruits. I woke my friends up and went out to look for Yusuf. Then he came in and he said, 'This is your lunch. Please help yourselves.'

We ate our lunch and drank tea, and then bade him farewell.

My colleagues got into the car while I stood thanking Yusuf. A tall lady who was moving her arms back and forth as she walked came up and said, 'A car arrived at the car park and the passengers inside it asked about your house. Who are they?'

Yusuf replied, 'They are the sons of the Shaikhs of Sharjah, guests of Reis al-Sa'di . . . and here they are, right in front of you.'

'This is indeed a new piece of news!' the tall lady said. 'Here's the rest of the news. So and so has had a new child, and so and so made a sale for fifty thousand . . . and so on.'

Then she left us.

I asked him, 'Who was that?'

He said, 'She is called "Ilm Dar". She is the daily newspaper in the town of Lar.'

We drove out of Lar before sunset that day.

After a few hours of driving in the mountains at night, we stopped in front of a group of officers from the Anti-Smuggling Centre who were on the lookout for contraband.

Dr Ja'far's brother got out of the car with his bag and headed towards the inspector. I followed him to hear what he was saying to them to make it easier for us to get through the checkpoints.

Dr Ja'far's brother said to the officers, 'These are important people . . . the sons of the Shaikhs of Sharjah . . . guests of the government.'

Dr Ja'far then took out the letter from my father to Major General Rahmani. After they read it, they saluted us and we went on in our car right in front of them.

After we had passed through the checkpoint, the car stopped by a shop at the side of the road. We bought some food but when we got back into the car we found that Marzuq and his assistant had not come back. We fell asleep.

When I woke up the car was swaying. I looked at the other side of the car and saw a light shining into a deep ravine. We were at the top of a mountain, and the road was narrow and winding. I looked through the glass dividing the front seat from the back and saw Marzuq and his assistant. They were drinking alcohol from a bottle they were sharing with each other. They were both drunk. I stood up and started banging on the front part of the roof of the car with both hands. The car came to a halt. I got down and opened the door of the car on the side that Marzuq was sitting. I asked him to get out of the car. I grabbed the keys and ordered him to sleep until the morning. I kept the keys with me until then.

In the morning, we saw that the distance between the deep ravine and the car was wide enough only for a single person to pass by. Our car moved down into another ravine, then went up another mountain. The road was very narrow and the corners very sharp, to the extent that we all got out of the car at every turn. The car would negotiate the turns by moving forward and reversing, while we stood ready behind the car with large rocks to put under the wheels so that they would not slip. We were saying, 'Back . . . back . . . back . . .'

Then we rolled the rocks behind the wheels saying, 'Stop . . . stop . . . stop . . .'

We arrived at noon at a town called Jahrum, still on our way to Shiraz. The air there was pleasant and the gardens were lush and green. In the middle of the town was a public park which had large, old trees. Under the trees there was a restaurant in the open air, where we had the most delicious grilled meat and other tasty food.

A wise man was once asked, 'Who is the best chef?' 'Hunger!' he answered.

Between Jahrum and Shiraz there is a region which is called Ali Abad where cantaloupes and watermelons are grown, and they are sold in abundance on the side of the road. Early that night, our car was stopped on the outskirts of the city of Shiraz at the Inspection Centre. We were all taken from the car except for a boy from Jahrum who was getting a ride with us. The car was put under guard. The boy woke up and wanted to go and urinate, but they wouldn't allow him. We were put in a room at the Inspection Centre. Dr Ja'far's brother called his uncle, who was the Chief of Police in Shiraz. His uncle ordered that the car be sent to the Directorate of Security in Shiraz with the people in the car under guard.

Our car left the Inspection Centre, leaving a damp spot under the car where the boy had been sitting, and passed through the streets of Shiraz with four soldiers standing in it, pointing their machine guns at us. We were sitting jammed up close to each other and whenever the car stopped at a corner or at a light, people gathered around to have a look.

At the Directorate of Security in Shiraz, Dr Ja'far's uncle received us. He let us into the city of Shiraz along with the car and the load it was carrying. Dr Ja'far's brother dropped us at the door of a modest hotel, and he disappeared with his boxes of smuggled goods.

We spent three days in Shiraz. We visited the city's landmarks and the Takht-e-Jamshid region, which is more than sixty kilometres from Shiraz. In that area are the ruins of Persepolis, dating from the Achaemenid period in the fifth century BC. There are columns there and a building carved from rocks of basalt, and a mural carved on it of the Achaemenid king with the peoples of the earth presenting gifts to him. I asked myself, 'Were our people, the Arabs, among those peoples who lived at the dawn of history?'

I looked over that picture, and I saw an Arab leading a camel.


## Tehran

On the fourth day, we rented a bus to take us from Shiraz to Tehran. On the way we visited Isfahan, where we had lunch on one of the banks of the Isfahan River. It was near the bridge which is estimated to be four hundred years old, and consists of thirty-three arches, after which it is named.

In Tehran, we stayed at a hotel on Parliament Square. The next day, we visited Mr Shahini, the owner and publisher of the *Itla'at* newspaper, who spoke fluent Arabic. He was a friend of Mr Ibrahim al-Midfa', the Minister of Shaikh Saqr bin Sultan al-Qasimi, the Ruler of Sharjah.

Mr Shahini arranged a meeting for us with Major General Rahmani, and I gave the letter from my father to him.

Mr Shahini visited us every day and used to have heated discussions with Taryam bin 'Umran, because, once again, the latter was fanatical in his support for Jamal Abdel Nasser, and the former was equally fervent in his love for the Shah of Iran.

Once we visited the Tehran Observatory. When Mr Shahini had visited us, he had asked, 'Have you visited the Tehran Observatory?'

Taryam bin 'Umran replied, 'In its time . . . the Helwan Observatory was the best.'

Mr Shahini leant over to me and asked, 'Where is the Helwan Observatory?'

'In Egypt!' I replied.

Mr Shahini said, 'I thought so!'

After the Shah's speech to the nation, Mr Shahin came to us and asked, 'Did you hear the Shah's speech?'

Taryam bin 'Umran replied, 'In its time, Abdel Nasser's speech was the best! The Shah's speech was only four words . . . Abdel Nasser's speech was four hours long.'

Mr Shahini remarked, 'The speech of kings . . . the kings of speech' (in this context 'kings of speech' means people who talk a lot of nonsense).

Mr Shanini was very stingy. He once invited us to have lunch in a hotel restaurant outside Tehran, where the bill was very expensive. We paid the bill from the funds set aside for our trip, which had begun to run low. The following evening, Mr Shahini came and told us that he had reserved a place for us to have dinner at one of the best restaurants in Tehran.

Muhammad al-Shamsi, our treasurer, objected. He said, 'Sultan and I won't be able to go with you as we are going to the cinema.'

Taryam bin 'Umran said, 'Sultan and Muhammad are going to the cinema, and my brother 'Abdullah, Ya'qub and I will go with you.'

After the great banquet, Taryam, Ya'qub and 'Abdullah returned and told us what had happened.

Taryam said, 'We ordered the most expensive food, and when the time to pay the bill came I said that I had to go to the bathroom. From there, I waved to 'Abdullah to come to me, as Mr Shahini had poor eyesight. 'Abdullah came and I kept waving my hand to Ya'qub until he came, too. We waited a long time watching Mr Shahini surreptitiously from the bathroom. He was looking around, trying to find us with his thick glasses. There were no other patrons in the restaurant and the owners of the restaurant started to hover around Mr Shahini . . . until finally he paid the bill.'

Taryam continued, 'After I returned with 'Abdullah and Ya'qub to the table, I clapped my hands and called, "The bill!"'

Mr Shahini said, 'That was some trick!'

Major General Rahmani requested a meeting with us. When he came to the hotel, he offered us the chance to return to Sharjah on board a plane that would be bringing the Shaikh of Umm al-Qaiwain to Tehran at the invitation of the Shah of Iran.

Taryam said, 'Sultan wants to take the train. We decided to go by train to Khorramshahr, and from there by the British India Steam Navigation Company to Sharjah. Sultan loves rail travel.'

Major General Rahmani said, 'We will arrange for you to travel by train to the Caspian Sea, and to stay there for a few days until the departure of the plane to Sharjah.'

## The Caspian Sea

Early the next morning after the meeting, two cars arrived at the hotel to take us to the railway station. There was a young Iranian man with the two cars, who said his name was Labbaf. He was to be our translator for the trip.

We got on the train, and as it moved out we were surprised to find the person in charge of the train standing in front of us. He screamed, 'Sultan . . . Taryam!'

He kissed us. He turned out to be the guest of my father who had been in Sharjah a few weeks earlier. My father had invited him along with his wife, who had been the personal nurse to my father when he was receiving treatment in Tehran. He, along with all the other workers on the train, gave us special treatment on our trip.

The trip took the whole day. All of us enjoyed the beautiful scenery, except for Taryam, who stayed in the cabin arguing with the translator Labbaf about the Shah of Iran's policies.

Finally, we pulled into the last railway station, Bandar Pahlavi, which is on the Caspian Sea. Before the port was built it was a town called Anzeli.

A Land-Rover was waiting for us there. It took us along the coastal route, and headed west to the city of Chaluz, on the Caspian coast. We stayed the night there in a multi-storey hotel. In the morning, we saw the sky filled with clouds that were very close to the ground, and drizzle was falling from them. We got into the car and headed west on the coastal road to a renowned resort called Ramser, where we arrived at noon. We stayed in a villa at the hotel, which was built in the hills about three kilometres from the sea.

On the second day, we went by car to the beach on a well-made road that extended from the gate of the hotel in the hills to the gate of the rest area on the beach, where there was a place for gambling. There was nothing on that road except for a statue of the Shah of Iran, which was halfway between the two places. Then we moved to the tea plantations and the factory for drying the tea.

On the third day, the car took us west down the coastal road. From there we went to the interior region, where we passed by the rice fields, the scent of which resembled that of boiled rice.

The driver of the car asked people on the way for the distance to Rasht. The farmers in the fields answered that it was forty-five kilometres . . . thirty kilometres . . . fifteen kilometres . . .

We eventually arrived at the city of Rasht. The streets were lined with orange trees, which at that time were full of fruit.

We left the city of Rasht after having lunch there, and headed north-west to a city on the Caspian coast called Astara. It was on the Russian–Iranian border, which is divided by a stream that comes down from the hills to the sea. Loudspeakers were installed on both banks of the stream: a group on the Russian side insulted the Shah's regime, while a group on the Iranian side insulted the Soviet regime.

Then we went back to Ramser.

On the fourth day, we returned to Tehran in the car that was with us, via Karaj. At the end of August 1959, we returned to Sharjah on board the Iranian plane that was taking Shaikh Ahmad bin Rashid al-Muʻalla to Tehran in response to the invitation of the Iranian government to the Shaikhs of the coast. A number of Shaikhs had gone earlier to visit Tehran. Shaikh Ahmad bin Rashid al-Muʻalla didn't get on the plane due to illness.

## Opening of the Israeli office in Tehran

At the beginning of September 1959, the Iranian government announced the opening of an Israeli office in Tehran. Demonstrations broke out in Bahrain in protest, while in Sharjah a protest broke out on the morning of 5 September 1959, led by Taryam bin ʻUmran and myself. The demonstration moved to Sharjah airport, where the Iranian plane that was going to take one of the Shaikhs to Tehran was due to arrive.

Soon the Iranian plane arrived and its door opened. Major General Rahmani peered out of the door; he waved both hands to the crowds led by me and Taryam bin ʻUmran, thinking that we had come to greet him, since he had taken care of us during our stay in Tehran. He called out to us, 'Sultan! Taryam!' The security men pushed him back into the plane but he resisted them, saying, 'They are my friends! They have come to greet me!'

9

*The Ba'ath Party*

IN SEPTEMBER 1959 I REOPENED the People's Sports and Cultural Club in Sharjah, which had been closed for four years. The club was originally established by a group of young people in 1952, and the Board of Directors comprised the following: Shaikh Khalid bin Sultan al-Qasimi, Shaikh Muhammad bin Sultan al-Qasimi, Shaikh Hamad bin Majid al-Qasimi, Shaikh Saqr bin Rashid al-Qasimi, Mr 'Abdullah bin Jum'a al-Mutawwa' and Mr Ibrahim bin 'Ubaid al-Sha'ir.

The club had been closed down in 1954 with the departure of Shaikh Khalid bin Sultan al-Qasimi for Saudi Arabia, and the appointment of Shaikh Muhammad bin Sultan al-Qasimi as the Deputy to the Ruler of the Eastern Region.

The activities of the club previously had been only cultural in nature. When I opened the club a second time in 1959, I made it the headquarters of the football team for the British Ministry of Public Works in Sharjah, of which I was a member after I had been appointed to the captaincy of the team.

People started to come to the club to meet each other or to

175

play dominoes or cards. Among those who would regularly visit the club was a teacher named Talal Shararah, a Lebanese teacher from the Qatar Education Mission at the Qasimiyyah School.

Because of Arab nationalism our friendship grew stronger. One day he gave me a book entitled *In the Pursuit of Ba'ath* by Michel Aflaq, which took me several days to read due to the large number of pages. When I'd finished reading it, he asked me, 'What did you think of the book?' I replied, 'A good book. If only all of the ideas in it would come true!'

Talal Shararah spent a whole month telling me about the idea that if there were an organisation in every Arab country, which came to power and integrated with units already organised in other Arab countries, the whole Arab nation would be united.

One day, he told me that this organisation was called the Ba'ath Party. The Party had become established in the Arab world, and he asked me to join it.

A few days later, Talal Shararah told me that he would register my membership in the Ba'ath Party. He took me to his house, where he told me, 'You must swear an oath. There are only two of us. There needs to be a third. Wait, I will bring a third member.' He left the room and returned, accompanied by Taryam bin 'Umran. We were stunned. A moment went by in silence. Taryam had joined before me, but he thought that I had joined before him.

The silence was broken by Talal Shararah, who said, 'Sultan will take the oath, and this will be witnessed by Taryam. Then Taryam will take the oath, and this will be witnessed by Sultan.' Then I held out my hand to shake his.

The last days of 1959 went by and 1960 arrived. Through

the pamphlets and books supplied to us by Talal Shararah, we absorbed the ideas of nationalism and a single unified culture and education.

## A Baʿathist cell revealed

In April 1960, Talal Shararah came to complain to me about an order that had been issued to him by the Department of Education in Qatar. His service was to be terminated at the end of the school term, and he told me that he would try to travel to Qatar to enquire about the matter personally. However, he was afraid that he would be detained in Qatar if he travelled on his Lebanese passport. I told him that I could get him a temporary passport from the Government of Sharjah, which I did.

I took Talal Shararah to Sharjah airport, and when he returned from Qatar after sunset the next day I met him and took him in my car to the Cultural Club in Sharjah.

On the way, Talal Shararah told me what he had heard from his friends in the Department of Education in Qatar. He said that Abd-Rabbu Saqr, Head of the Qatar Education Mission in Sharjah, had written a report about him saying that he, Talal, had created a Baʿathist cell among the teachers. Abd-Rabbu Saqr had hidden among them to reveal the activities of Party member Talal and other teachers in the Mission whose contracts had been terminated along with that of Talal.

Once the car reached the club, Talal Shararah got out in a rage. He rushed towards Abd-Rabbu Saqr, who was sitting next to Taryam bin ʿUmran. I grabbed him and asked him to sit in the car so that I could bring Taryam bin ʿUmran and Abd-Rabbu

Saqr to him. We could then take them to his house, where we could ask Abd-Rabbu Saqr about the matter.

I brought Taryam and Abd-Rabbu Saqr to the car, and we all went to Talal Shararah's house. Once we'd entered the yard of the house, Talal Shararah started beating Abd-Rabbu Saqr with his shoe. Although Taryam and I managed to stop the fight, the loud insults continued in the yard. I asked Abd-Rabbu Saqr if he was the one who had revealed the cell of teachers and he denied it. I then asked him, 'How do you explain the sacking of all the members of the cell except for you?' Abd-Rabbu Saqr stuttered and was unable to answer. So Talal Shararah promptly kicked him out of his house.

At the end of the school year, the end of May 1960, the teachers left. Those who could not travel stayed behind because they had local contracts. Among those who left was Talal Shararah, who told me that he would settle his affairs in Qatar and go to Lebanon. Talal gave me his address in Lebanon and a writing communication code through the owner of the barber's shop in front of the religious court in Doha in Qatar.

One of the teachers who left for Qatar was Abd-Rabbu Saqr. News came to me by way of Ba'athist sources that Abd-Rabbu Saqr was going to stay in Qatar and would not be travelling to Gaza because he was afraid that he would be assassinated there.

After a few days, news came to me from the same source that a truck had run over Abd-Rabbu Saqr on the pavement of a street in Doha. I was filled with suspicion.

## *The Shuwaikh Secondary School*

After the completion of my second year studies at the Qasimiyyah School, it was decided that I would complete my studies in the third and fourth forms at the Shuwaikh Secondary School in Kuwait.

Ever since I'd been at the Qasimiyyah School, until I moved to Kuwait, I was top of the class. I joined in all the student activities. I was the First Sergeant of the two Scout groups, I was the captain of the school's football team and I joined in the sports festivals, in which I always competed in six events. I was the first in the 100-metre sprint, second in the 400 metres, second in the 800 metres, second in the high jump, first in the long jump and first in the hurdles.

As for cultural activities I produced a weekly wall magazine in Arabic, called *Al-Taqaddum* (Progress), and another in English, called *Progress*. I wrote all the articles for both magazines myself. Among my artistic activities I submitted a painting and a display for each annual exhibition: one display was about methods of irrigation and another was about activities in oil production. I also drew the illustrations for all the school's grade levels from elementary to secondary.

When I moved to Shuwaikh Secondary School in September 1960 we were based in house number 12, so I sent this information to Doha, adding that a new comrade had joined us whose name was 'Abdullah bin Salim al-'Umrani. He was with us in the same class. The Ba'athist cell, which consisted of the student Sultan bin Muhammad al-Qasimi, as head of the cell, comrade student Taryam bin 'Umran bin Taryam and comrade student

'Abdullah bin Salim al-'Umrani, also relocated. One evening after we had arrived in house number 12, we were visited by a person named Mohammed al-Ramlawi who had two other people with him. When Mohammed al-Ramlawi asked for 'Abdullah bin Muhammad al-Qasimi, I replied, 'I am Sultan bin Muhammad al-Qasimi.'

'We want your brother,' he said.

'My brother is not here,' I told him.

Then he asked about Sultan bin Salim al-'Umrani.

I told him, 'His name is 'Abdullah bin Salim al-'Umrani.'

Then he asked for Taryam bin 'Umran.

I got Taryam for him . . . and he took him aside.

After speaking with him, they returned to us and Taryam said to him, 'This is *Sultan* bin Muhammad al-Qasimi and this is *'Abdullah* bin Salim al-'Umrani.'

Mohammed Al-Ramlawi said, 'I am a member of the Ba'ath Party. I have come to arrange your affairs in Kuwait so that you attend the meetings without any problems. The first meeting is on Thursday evening.'

On a Thursday evening in September 1960 the three of us, Taryam bin 'Umran, 'Abdullah bin Salim al-'Umrani and I, got into a taxi at the front gate of the Shuwaikh Secondary School. The taxi let us out at the taxi stand near Safah. A few steps away was a café, where we drank tea and waited for a reasonable amount of time. Then we got into another taxi which took us to the Hawli Summer Cinema, in the Hawli area.

We sat in the restaurant of the cinema and ordered some food. When the box office opened, the people went to buy tickets. We got into the queue with the other people, and kept ourselves apart from each other. When one of us in the queue got close to the entrance of the cinema, we left the queue and headed to the side of the cinema, which was in complete darkness. We found Mohammed al-Ramlawi waiting there for us so that he could accompany us through the dark streets of Hawli to a house where we met an Iraqi named Mohammed Sa'id. He said that he had just returned from Brazil.

For several weeks we were like that, living in anticipation and fear, in disguise and with deception. This was until the subject of allegations against Jamal Abdel Nasser came up during a meeting. When this happened Taryam flew into a rage against Mohammed Sa'id, asking him, 'Is this your personal opinion, or the opinion of the leadership?!'

Mohammed Sa'id answered, 'This is the opinion of the leadership.'

When Taryam decided to leave the house of Mohammed Sa'id, Mohammed al-Ramlawi tried to stop him. However, with his determination and our support, we were able to get out and return to Kuwait City.

## Withdrawal from the Ba'ath Party

The three of us agreed to withdraw from the Ba'ath Party. 'Abdullah bin Salim al-'Umrani left his studies and travelled to Sharjah after receiving news of the death of his father. Taryam bin 'Umran started to go with a group including his brother 'Abdullah and Sa'id al-Sha'ir to visit his uncles every Thursday and Friday in the Sha'biyya neighbourhood in Ahmadi.

As for me, every Thursday evening I would wait for a taxi in front of the Shuwaikh Secondary School to go to Kuwait City. One Thursday as I was waiting for a taxi it got late, so I walked beside the wall of the school towards Kuwait City. A car stopped and two people got out. They asked me to get in and talk to Mr Mohammed al-Ramlawi. I looked around me. The Industrial School was in front of me, and on the other side of the road the school buildings were separated from the road by a large number of tamarisk trees. Behind me were the houses of the teachers who worked at the Shuwaikh Secondary School, which were some distance from the wall. There were no pedestrians or cars on the street.

Mohammed al-Ramlawi called to me: 'Sultan . . . Get in. We will give you a lift.'

'I am waiting for my friends,' I replied.

'Get in,' he said. 'I want to talk to you.'

The passenger door was open. I leant in to talk to Mohammed al-Ramlawi. Behind me stood his two companions, who wanted to close the door. Having concluded that he had good intentions, I got into the car. His bodyguards sat in the back seat.

We talked for the entire journey from Shuwaikh to Kuwait City without mentioning the subject of the Ba'ath Party. I was relaxed until we arrived at Kuwait City. The car turned right to take the ring road.

'Where are we going?' I asked.

He said, 'Mohammed Sa'id wants to talk with you.'

I put my fate in the hands of God.

We arrived in Hawli City and went to the house of Mohammed Sa'id, who was frowning. He poured scorn on me, and said I was the one who had urged Taryam and 'Abdullah not to attend.

I apologised for that, and tried to explain without going into the issue of Jamal Abdel Nasser. But to no avail. There were two of them along with the two men from the car. Night was falling. I was afraid that I would be buried alive in the yard of the house. I swore by my honour, as this was their oath, although I was deceiving them, that I would start coming again from the following Thursday.

I asked permission to leave. Mohammed al-Ramlawi tried to leave with me, but I swore by God that he would not do so.

After I left the house, I ran as fast as I could so that no one could follow me. As soon as I arrived at the Hawli Summer Cinema, I immediately hailed a taxi to take me to the Shuwaikh Secondary School. The following week, I didn't go to the meeting.

In the middle of that week, I went to Kuwait to get my shoes mended. The devils of the Ba'ath Party knew that students were not permitted to go out during weekdays, except on Thursday and Friday. I took a taxi from the gate of the Shuwaikh Secondary School, and got out near Safah. I asked about the shop which mended shoes and sandals and was told that it was towards the end of the Gharabally Market, in the direction of Salihiyya.

In the Gharabally Market, I bumped into Mohammed al-Ramlawi.

'*Al-salamu 'alaikum,*' I said.

'*Wa 'alaikum al-salam . . .*' he replied. 'Where are you going?'

'To fix my shoes,' I replied.

'I'll come with you,' he said.

'There's no need for that.'

'You left us waiting last Thursday evening. You didn't turn up. You swore on your honour that you would come.'

'Listen, Mohammed al-Ramlawi,' I replied, 'tell Mohammed Sa'id that I will not belong to an organisation that makes a mockery of unity, which was the reason we entered the Ba'ath Party in the first place. I won't be a member of a party that insults Jamal Abdel Nasser, who is a symbol of that unity. We will not tolerate those insults.'

He responded, 'Sultan, by God you are dear to me. I fear for you. These people . . .'

'What?' I said. 'By God I will have you for lunch before you have me for dinner. Do you see this policeman?' I asked, indicating a traffic policeman. 'Through him I can expose all the elements of the Ba'ath Party in Kuwait, as well as in Qatar and Sharjah. I have a family that will protect me, but you all . . .'

He cut me off, threatening, 'Where is Abd-Rabbu Saqr? Put all this aside and let's remain friends,' he added.

'May God's curse be upon you all,' I said angrily, and left him. I couldn't believe what I had just heard.

On Thursday evening that same week, I got in the car with one of my friends to go to Kuwait. I asked the driver to let me out in the Mirqab district, where I intended to meet a friend of mine, Rashid bin 'Ali bin Dimas. He was from Sharjah and was working in Kuwait. I wanted to go with him to the shop where my shoes were being mended.

I found the house of Rashid bin Dimas locked so I sat in a café called the Somalis' Café, in front of Rashid bin Dimas' house, so that if he came back I would see him. A long time went by. When it was almost sunset, I caught a glimpse of someone who looked like Mohammed Al-Ramlawi among the crowds in the café. I was overcome with fear. I told myself I had to get out of that place. I headed to the Shamlan Mosque in Abdullah al-Mubarak Square.

The road to the mosque was wide and paved with asphalt. To the right of the road was open ground where some of the houses in Mirqab had been demolished. I was walking in front of the houses that had not been demolished when suddenly I heard a voice in front of me calling, 'Watch out! Watch out!'

I turned . . . A car travelling at high speed tried to knock me down. I jumped onto the ruins of some old walls, and the car drove by without touching me. The Egyptian man who had warned me said, 'That car didn't have a registration number.' I was really scared.

After the sunset prayer in the Shamlan Mosque, I met Rashid bin Dimas and went with him to collect my shoes before returning to Rashid's house for the night.

## Leaving school in Kuwait

On the morning of Friday 23 December 1960, I went with Rashid bin Dimas to the Shuwaikh Secondary School. I packed my bag and went back with Rashid bin Dimas to his house, where again I stayed the night.

The next morning, I went with Rashid bin Dimas to the Department of Education where I received my passport. That night I could not sleep as I waited anxiously to leave Kuwait in the morning. I prayed to God:

*Oh Lord, decrease my suffering and be merciful;*
*the young man has repented.*
*What have I done during my life for the dream to have turned into*
  *a mirage?*
*Where have I spent my days and my youth?*
*(I say to myself) Don't ask! I have lost them.*
*Oh my Lord, forgive me and don't blame me;*
*I have lost my sense of direction.*
*How many of those who are ignorant of you live frivolous lives, and*
  *then wake up? And to you we all return.*

On the morning of Sunday 25 December 1960, I took a plane from Kuwait to Dhahran in Saudi Arabia. I stayed a few weeks in the city of Khobar and visited my sister 'Alia, her husband Shaikh Salim bin Sultan al-Qasimi, an engineer on the railway in Dammam, and their children. I then returned to Sharjah.

IO

*The Sharjah Trade School Teacher*

AFTER I HAD RETURNED FROM Saudi Arabia in February 1961, I found that my cousins, Shaikh Khalid and Shaikh Muhammad, the sons of my uncle, the late Shaikh Sultan al-Qasimi, had returned to Sharjah. The dispute between them and their brother Shaikh Saqr bin Sultan al-Qasimi, the Ruler of Sharjah, had ended and they got involved in business that took them far away from the problems of government.

One day, Shaikh Muhammad bin Sultan al-Qasimi asked me to work with him in some business, but I declined. The next day, Shaikh Khalid bin Sultan al-Qasimi visited me. He offered me a position at Sharjah airport, but I declined this offer as well. Two days after that visit, he came to offer me another job as a teacher in the Sharjah Trade School. This time I accepted.

'Let's go now!' he said.

'Now?' I asked.

He said, 'Yes. The headmaster, Mr John Taylor, is waiting for us!'

Shaikh Khalid took me to the school in Sharjah, where we met Mr Taylor who was a man of impeccable manners. After we had spoken, Mr Taylor said to Shaikh Khalid, 'Leave Sultan with us. We will take him home whenever he wants.'

After Shaikh Khalid had left, Mr Taylor said to me, 'Consider yourself an employee from the first of the month.'

I started teaching English and mathematics at the school. Every morning Mr Taylor passed by the classroom to say hello. He would stand listening to me as I explained the lesson. He would turn the pages of my lecture notes to see what was being taught to the students. Then he would leave.

One day, as he was looking through my notes he was surprised at what he saw. Some of the pages in the book were wrinkled and torn, and a substance had leaked over the pages, smudging the writing!

'What's this?!' he asked.

I said, 'Let's go outside the classroom.'

When we were outside, I said, 'As I was locking the door to my house, I put the book containing my lecture notes on the bench beside the door. A goat came along and took the book. I ran after it while it was carrying the book in its mouth. It ran from one street to another, until it got to the house it came from. The door to the house was open, so the goat went inside. I stood at the door calling, "Grab the goat!"

'"What do you want?" asked the lady of the house.'

The goat was standing in the middle of the yard of the house. It was looking at me and chewing my lecture notes, shaking its head and gloating. I immediately jumped onto the goat and brought it to the ground, forcing open its jaws to release my book. Mr Taylor laughed at my story.

I worked at that school for two and a half years, from February 1961 to September 1963. During that time, several major events happened in Sharjah.

## The death of my father

In the middle of March 1962, my sister Na'ima and I decided to spend two days in Ras al-Khaimah. She came with a group of women. As soon as we arrived at Ras al-Khaimah, I got a strange feeling, urging me to go to my father. I told my sister, 'I'm going back to Sharjah.'

'We agreed that we would stay in Ras al-Khaimah and go back tomorrow,' she said.

'You stay here with the driver,' I said. 'I'll go back to Sharjah by taxi.'

'Why?' she asked.

'I don't know!' I replied.

In the taxi all I could think about was my father. As we passed by the centre of Jazirat al-Hamra, the driver was told that Shaikh Saqr bin Sultan al-Qasimi, the Ruler of Sharjah, had been on his way to Ras al-Khaimah when a car coming from Ras al-Khaimah had stopped him in the middle of Jazirat al-Hamra. After that he had returned to Sharjah immediately. Nobody knew what had been said to Shaikh Saqr bin Sultan al-Qasimi.

I said to myself that something serious must have happened. When we arrived in Sharjah, I looked at the shops near the Rolla tree thinking to myself that, if they were open, I would feel relief; but if they were closed, it meant an important person must have died. All of the shops were closed.

191

I told the taxi driver, 'Let me out here.'

I walked to our house. It was quiet and dark. When I entered my father's room, I looked at the bed on which he slept. It was empty. I buried my face in the covers and cried.

My father had been suffering from partial paralysis as a result of a stroke in his brain that had occurred while he was receiving treatment in Beirut for his broken leg in February 1959.

In November 1959, he had suffered a second stroke and had been taken immediately to Bahrain. From there he had been taken to Bombay, where he had recovered.

My father had passed away that morning. A funeral had been held for him and he had been buried, while I had been far away. He was fifty-four years old when he died.

## Shaikh Saqr bin Sultan al-Qasimi, the Ruler of Sharjah, and his brothers

After Shaikh Saqr bin Sultan al-Qasimi returned from his tour of Europe, on Thursday 6 September 1962, he found that his brothers were plotting against him.

On Monday 10 September 1962, Shaikh Saqr bin Sultan al-Qasimi ordered the police to arrest all his brothers except Ahmad, who was too young. That night the police arrested and imprisoned Shaikh Khalid bin Sultan, Shaikh 'Abdullah bin Sultan and Shaikh Sa'ud bin Sultan.

Shaikh Muhammad bin Sultan and his brother, Shaikh Salim bin Sultan, returned from Dubai that night. When Shaikh Muhammad bin Sultan arrived at his house, he found policemen surrounding it. So he returned with his brother to Dubai.

In the middle of that night, Shaikh 'Abdullah bin Sultan al-Qasimi was released. Shaikh Khalid and Shaikh Sa'ud remained in prison until the morning, when they were deported by plane to Qatar.

## The unification of Egypt, Syria and Iraq

On Wednesday 17 April 1963, a tripartite agreement was signed between the Republic of Iraq and the United Arab Republic (Egypt and Syria) unifying the three countries. People throughout the Arab world were overjoyed. In the emirates, their joy quickly became tinged with sorrow at subsequent events.

In Ras al-Khaimah, on the evening of Thursday 18 April 1963, the day after the signing of the tripartite agreement, a party was held in the evening for the wedding of the Ruler's son, Shaikh Khalid bin Saqr bin Muhammad al-Qasimi. I was with those who were there watching the festivities. My aunt, Shaikha Mira bint Muhammad al-Suwaidi, who was the widow of Shaikh Sultan bin Saqr al-Qasimi and grandmother of the groom, had asked me to take her and a group of women in my car to Ras al-Khaimah for the wedding party.

In front of the Ras al-Khaimah Fort, a simple stage was set up. It was constructed of palm branches so that singers could sing along to the traditional bands. Among those who sang there that night were Mr Ibrahim Shuma, the music teacher at the Qasimiyyah School in Sharjah. Most of the songs were patriotic songs, including a new song about the city of Cairo and its famous tower of Al-Jazira. The song started with:

*At the top of Al-Jazira Tower*
*O Lord, how charming it is!*

On the way into the city of Ras al-Khaimah there was a tower near the Jazirat al-Hamra cemetery, which is called the Al-Jazira Tower. From the top you could see the town of Ras al-Khaimah. Although he was singing about the tower in Cairo, the people thought that Mr Ibrahim Shuma was singing about Ras al-Khaimah and gave him lots of money.

Shaikh Saqr bin Muhammad al-Qasimi, the Ruler of Ras al-Khaimah, was later reprimanded by A. J. M. Craig, the British Political Resident, because of this. The British at the time perceived the unification as a step that would strengthen Egypt's position under Jamal Abdel Nasser who had been the powerful symbol of the new Arab nationalism.

On the evening of the third day after the signing of the tripartite agreement, Friday 19 April 1963, when Shaikh Saqr bin Sultan al-Qasimi, the Ruler of Sharjah, was out of the country, I went out to lead a large demonstration in support of the tripartite agreement. I took the demonstrators to the football stadium near the perimeter fence of Sharjah airport, between the Cultural Club and the taxi station. The demonstration in support of the unification of Egypt, Syria and Iraq included old people and young, women and children. Among the women was an elderly lady called Amina bint 'Ali, who was also known as Manuh Hara'iq. She had hung a picture of Jamal Abdel Nasser on her chest. This was not the first time she had done this. She even used to ask the British soldiers when they came to the Sharjah Market to greet 'Nasser' and his picture on her chest.

That evening, she asked a person who was passing by in the demonstration to greet Jamal Abdel Nasser. However, instead of greeting him, this person spat at the picture. Manuh Hara'iq screamed, 'Grab him! Beat him! He spat on the picture of Abdel Nasser!'

A group of demonstrators ran after the man who had spat on the picture of Abdel Nasser. However, he got into a white saloon car that was parked by the fence of the airport and locked the doors. The demonstrators started rocking the car until they overturned it and it lay on its back. Someone opened the petrol tank of the car and the petrol spilled over the ground. He set it on fire and the car started to burn. A fire engine from the airport rushed to the burning car and a hose was pointed at it. However, the demonstrators began pelting the fire engine with stones, forcing it to withdraw. Although the fire was put out, all that was left of the car was a metal shell. We did not find the body of the man, as he had fled before the car had been set on fire.

The next day, 20 April 1963, I returned home from the Trade School in Sharjah and found my brother, Shaikh 'Abdul 'Aziz bin Muhammad al-Qasimi, standing in his military uniform waiting for me. He was an officer in the Trucial Oman Scouts and had come to warn me not to hold any more demonstrations. He informed me that the soldiers of the TOS had spread out everywhere, and that they had orders to put a stop to any demonstration. As arrangements had been made for a demonstration that afternoon, I went to the place where the demonstrators were ready to move. I stopped them and explained to them that the British intended to use force to stop the demonstration.

Voices around me shouted, 'Are you afraid? We are not afraid. Let them do whatever they want!'

I told them that we had women, children and elderly people with us. We did not want this demonstration to turn into a confrontation, but to express our happiness for the unity agreement.

After everyone had dispersed, I recited the following verses:

> *My country, if time betrays*
> *Or if the occupiers want to fight you*
> *I wish you peace*
> *My country, we have lived many years*
> *Years that have revealed a blazing fire*
> *Our obedience to the occupiers is not humility*
> *And our silence with them is not respect*
> *But fear of violence*
> *It is like the firewood gatherer at night blaming the darkness*
> *The widows appear sombre*
> *And elders become – in their hands – wreckage*
> *The baby crawls to the breast of his mother*
> *From her face they tear off a veil*
> *My country, if time betrays you, then keep saying*
> *Peace . . . Peace . . . Peace*

A few days later in Dubai, on the evening of 23 April, a party was held at the boys' school located to the east of the National Cinema to celebrate the announcement of the unity agreement, and some political speeches were made. When the party was over, the students left in a procession, passing between the town quarter and the National Cinema, and entering the square in front of the cinema. A small group of Iranians attacked them there. Nobody knew why. Perhaps because the relations between Egypt's Nasser and Iran's Shah were strained at the time. One of the students was killed and a number of others were wounded.

The next evening, after leaving the Trade School, I made my way to Dubai to enquire about what had happened the day before. I met Mr Batti bin Bishr, who told me of the events.

He said, 'There were crowds in front of the Dubai Police Headquarters, shouting threats and calling for revenge. The threats were directed at the British officer in the Dubai police who had detained the person accused of the murder. They demanded that he hand over the man to them so that they could kill him. The demonstration did not subside until Mr Saif bin Ahmad al-Ghurair – a Dubai merchant who was at the demonstration – intervened. He spoke to the angry demonstrators and they listened to his advice.'

Mr Batti went on: 'It has been said that Saif bin Ahmad al-Ghurair participated that morning in the funeral of the demonstrator who had been killed, and that he also helped in the burial of that demonstrator. He raised his hands after finishing the burial and prayed loudly for the deceased.'

The crowd was dispersed and the accused remained in police custody. He was later tried, convicted and sentenced to life imprisonment.

As we were talking, another group of demonstrators arrived. Mr Batti bin Bishr and I joined in and headed towards the Dubai Police Headquarters. But before it arrived there, a group of Dubai police blocked the way of the demonstrators.

At that moment Mr Thani bin 'Abdullah Abu Qafl, a prominent person in Dubai, intervened and tried to calm the protestors
down. However, the protestors started jostling the police, prompt-
ing them to use their batons. The demonstrators then dispersed,
except for a small group that stayed and continued to shout. Mr
Batti bin Bishr and myself were among the people in that small
group. Some policemen pursued us until we were near the house
of Khalifa bin Sultan al-Habtur, and finally the group dispersed.
Mr Batti bin Bishr and I went down the narrow lane which led to
the Deira Market, but in the middle of the lane we were followed
by one of the policemen, a man named Ahmad Hadid.

Ahmad Hadid, who was lightly built, started quarrelling with
Batti bin Bishr, who was very tall and strong. During the alterca-
tion, the 'iqal (head cord) of Ahmad Hadid fell down around his
neck. Batti bin Bishr handed me one end of the 'iqal, and started
hitting Ahmad Hadid with his hands.

I freed the policeman from the grip of Batti bin Bishr and
we continued on our way down the lane until we reached the
shore of Dubai Creek, where we found Thani bin 'Abdullah Abu
Qafl, along with a small group of Dubai police to our right, and
another group of police on the left. The police attacked us. All
we could do was jump into an empty ferry boat which Mr Batti
bin Bishr rowed out into the middle of the Creek.

The killer was tried and found guilty, and the mother of the
murdered man was left to decide between retribution or *diyyah*
(blood money/compensation).

The enthusiasm for the United Arab Republic, which came
about with the signing of the tripartite agreement, was inde-
scribable. It was not only students and citizens who supported

Jamal Abdel Nasser. The flag of the United Arab Republic was flown from taxis, buildings and ferry boats that crossed back and forth over Dubai Creek, and on the ships that were anchored there. Loud shouts were heard coming from the mouths of the foreign taxi drivers, Baluchis on the boats and Pakistanis on the merchant ships: 'Nasser . . . Nasser . . .'

The British knew for certain then that everyone supported Nasser.

## Leg injury

I had been on the Qasimiyyah School football team. Once the Sharjah team played with a British team from the airport, and one of the players in the Sharjah team was missing. As there were no reserve players on the team, I was asked to play. I was fifteen years old at the time. I kept playing with that team until 1960, when I went to pursue my studies in Kuwait.

When I returned from Kuwait in 1961, I established the *Ittifaq Team*. It lasted for two years, until I closed it down as most of the players at that time were foreigners. At the beginning of 1963, I established al-Sha'b (the people's) club. It was in one of the club's matches that I sustained a fracture at the end of my tibia and I was forced to stop playing.

## Resignation from the Trade School
## in Sharjah and a return to study

At the end of May 1963, after the school year had been completed at the Trade School, I went to Cairo. From there I went to

Alexandria to meet Dr Muhammad 'Abdullah, an osteopathic physician, and told him about my leg. He told me after examination and X-rays that treatment would be useless as the bone had already set.

I subsequently returned to Cairo, as I had an inflamed appendix. There I had to go to hospital for surgery to remove the appendix.

When I met my classmates in Cairo, in the summer of 1963, all of them were at the end of their first year of studies at the University of Cairo. Memories of the past came back. We had been in the same class together for ten years. They asked me to stay with them in Cairo and to continue my studies at the Police College, following the programme for students from the east; that is, joining with a mid-level certificate. I promised them that I would follow them, but only after I had received the high school certificate. (I did not complete the high school certificate when I went to Kuwait in 1960. I had to leave in December of that year after what seemed to be life-threatening experiences during my encounters with some members of the Ba'ath Party there.)

After I returned to Sharjah, I sent my letter of resignation to the head of the Trade School in Sharjah, Mr Michael Burton, the Assistant British Political Agent in Dubai. He had been running the Trade School in Sharjah since the end of the previous school year, while the Director of the school was still getting treatment in Britain following an operation.

I presented my certificate to the Kuwait Office in Dubai to join the Dubai Secondary School, in the third form science stream. The third and fourth form science and humanities streams were divided between the Dubai Secondary School, which took the third and fourth forms for the science stream, and the Qasimiyyah School in Sharjah, which took the third and fourth forms for the humanities stream.

It was only a matter of days before the Deputy British Political Agent, Mr Burton, asked me to come and meet him at the British Political Residency in Dubai.

When I met Mr Burton, he was kind to me. He asked me to reconsider my resignation and go back to the school to teach.

I said, 'I am in the Dubai Secondary School continuing my education.'

'We will send you on a scholarship to study in Britain,' he replied.

I responded, 'So many promises have already been made and not kept!'

He said, 'Are we liars?'

'Interpret that in whatever way you want,' I replied.

He said, 'Before you went to Egypt you were polite and well-mannered, according to how Mr Taylor described you. But since you have been with the Egyptians you have been become rude.'

I said, 'If plain honesty is rudeness then may God increase this in me.'

He replied, 'I forbid you to resign.'

'You can't even stop me from leaving your office!' I said.

II

*Arab Nationalism Sweeps Sharjah*

B Y THE LATE 1950S AND early 1960s the tide of Arab nationalism, along with the influence of the Egyptian President
Nasser, spread around the Arab world including the Gulf
region. In Sharjah and Dubai the ideology of Arab nationalism was supported by different groups in society: the general
public, students, merchants and prominent people from Sharjah
and Dubai. This tide also spread to the Government of Sharjah,
which was represented by Shaikh Saqr bin Sultan al-Qasimi, the
Ruler.

## A play: Zionist Agents

At the end of 1963, and when I was a student at the Dubai
Secondary School, I was still managing the Cultural Club in
Sharjah. A wooden stage was built there during my time away in
Egypt in the summer of 1963. The first play to be performed on
the stage was in August 1963, and another play was performed in
September of the same year, staged by the Iraqi director Wathiq

al-Samara'i. For my part, I wrote a play entitled *Zionist Agents*, which I also directed and in which I played the two main roles. It was performed at the end of 1963.

The inner courtyard of the club where the stage was located was filled with the audience; sitting in the first row next to the stage was Mr Michael Burton, the Deputy British Political Agent in Dubai, and the Head of the Sharjah Trade School. He was sitting with 'Ubaid bin Ya'qub, Head of Transport at the school, whom I had also invited along with Mr Burton to attend the performance.

In the final act of the play, there was a scene in which Moshe Dayan, the Israeli Chief of Staff in the 1950s, appeared. I played the role of Dayan, in which I addressed the British Foreign Office in London. The conversation between Moshe Dayan (MD) and the British Foreign Office (BFO) went like this:

MD (on the telephone): Hello . . . Hello . . . London, the British Foreign Office!

BFO (on the telephone): Hello . . . Hello . . . Who is speaking?

MD: It's Moshe Dayan. The Arabs have launched an attack. Help us! Intervene! Stop them!

BFO: We can't do anything. The Arabs are now united and powerful. To intervene would be contrary to our interests in the region.

Then Moshe Dayan put down the telephone and moved to the edge of the stage, dangling his legs over the edge of its wooden boards. He directed his speech to Mr Michael Burton, the Deputy British Political Agent in Dubai, who was sitting in front of him. 'You created us, and you have made us a cat's paw for your interests. We were comfortable in the countries we lived in, and you gathered us up from every country and made us a tool of your aggression.'

The Deputy British Political Agent was angry that such a speech should be directed at him, and the next day he asked Shaikh Saqr bin Sultan al-Qasimi to close the Cultural Club. Following strong insistence by the British, he agreed to the request, and closed the club.

## The mission of the League of Arab States

In the spring of 1964, the Arab press launched a campaign against the threat of Iranian immigration to the Gulf emirates, due to the perceived threat this posed to the Arab identity of the region. After visiting the region in the summer of that year, the Ambassador at the Ministry of Foreign Affairs in Kuwait, Badr Khalid, had prepared a report on the region. He put the matter into its true perspective, commenting on the urgent need in the region for help and support

In October 1964, the Secretary-General of the League of Arab States, 'Abdul Khaliq Hassuna, announced that he would head a mission to establish formal relations between the Gulf States and the League of Arab States, and to study ways to preserve Arab identity. It was decided that the visit would begin on 28 October 1964.

For a week, Sharjah had been putting up flags and arches. On this day, Dubai too had become a most beautiful sight, filled with decorations. Work continued with raising flags and installing arches until dawn, before the delegation arrived. Decorations were also put up in other emirates.

That morning, about three thousand people from Dubai and other emirates gathered at Dubai airport, along with people of other nationalities.

The plane carrying 'Abdul Khaliq Hassuna arrived at precisely ten o'clock that morning. He disembarked from the plane along with his accompanying delegation. This comprised Sayyid Nufal, the Deputy Secretary-General of the League of Arab States, along with representatives to the League from Saudi Arabia, Kuwait and Iraq. Shaikh Rashid bin Sa'id al-Maktoum, the Ruler of Dubai, received them. The crowds of people pushed and shoved each other, and the police had to intervene to protect the visiting delegation. After having some refreshments at Dubai airport, the delegation went to their hotel in Dubai.

There was a small demonstration in support of the visit of the delegation by about twenty people accompanied by the Dubai police, at the hotel where the delegation was staying. That number grew to a hundred, and some of the demonstrators began to behave badly. This resulted in the police directing the demonstrators to an area of open ground near the hotel where there were some closed shops. The police, under orders from the British, then dispersed the demonstrators with batons, and the demonstrators responded in kind by pelting them with stones.

Perhaps the members of the delegation could not see what was happening behind the hotel, but they saw the cars packed with Yemeni workers and some students who had come from Sharjah. They shouted 'Victory to Jamal Abdel Nasser!' and 'Down with imperialism!' During the two days the delegation spent in Dubai, they were honoured with banquets and tea parties hosted by the Ruler of Dubai, Shaikh Rashid bin Sa'id al-Maktoum, the Kuwait Office in Dubai, and the Dubai Municipality. Finally, the delegation was hosted by Shaikh Ahmad bin 'Ali Al Thani, the Ruler of Qatar.

On 30 October 1964 the delegation visited Sharjah, where the Trucial Oman Scouts had deployed over the entire city. Most of the cars in Sharjah went to Dubai to join the delegation from Sharjah. I went with a group of demonstrators to meet the procession on the outskirts of the city. I talked to the crowds through a megaphone, while on top of one of the processing cars as far as the entrance to the guest house, where the *majlis* of Shaikh Saqr bin Sultan al-Qasimi, the Ruler of Sharjah, was located.

There were school students there, whose teachers directed them to shout and wave flags. The square in front of the guest house and the fort was crowded with citizens from Sharjah. Among them were Arabs from other countries as well as some Baluchi and Iranian workers.

The delegation held a meeting with Shaikh Saqr bin Sultan al-Qasimi, and the subject under discussion was the assistance that was needed. Shaikh Saqr mentioned that the Saudi representative to the League of Arab States, who was among those in the delegation, had presented him with an invitation from King Faisal bin 'Abdul-'Aziz Al Su'ud to visit the Kingdom of Saudi Arabia. He accepted this invitation.

After the discussions, the delegation moved to the house which had been prepared for them. This house was called the Hassuna House, and it was located near the Rolla tree.

After a short rest, Shaikh Saqr bin Sultan al-Qasimi went to the Hassuna House and took the delegation to attend the Friday prayer in the new mosque that had been built by 'Ali bin 'Abdullah al-'Uwais. The mosque was in front of the Sharjah Trade School. After finishing the prayers, Shaikh Saqr provided lunch for the delegation, and then the delegation rested in the Hassuna House. This was followed by a tea party hosted by the Sharjah Municipality.

That evening, Shaikh Saqr bin Sultan held a large banquet for the delegation, inviting all the dignitaries from around the region. After dinner, a closed meeting was held between members of the Arab League and Shaikh Saqr, after they had said farewell to the other guests who had been invited to the banquet. Shaikh Saqr accompanied his guests to the Hassuna House, where they spent the night.

In the morning of Saturday 31 October 1964, the delegation from the Arab League went to 'Ajman, where they were received by Shaikh Rashid bin Humaid al-Nu'aimi, the Ruler of 'Ajman, and a large crowd of citizens who had started shouting declarations against Iran. Secretary-General 'Abdul Khaliq Hassuna talked with Shaikh Rashid and asked him to tell his people not to shout things against any country, as all countries were friends to the League of Arab States. The delegation returned from 'Ajman directly to Dubai, where they were to stay. In the following three days the delegation visited the emirates of Umm al-Qaiwain, Ras al-Khaimah and Fujairah. On 4 November 1964 the delegation departed from Dubai airport.

The agreement between the delegation from the Arab League and the rulers of the emirates was to send a Technical Mission to study the region's needs with regard to necessary projects.

## *Technical Arab support*

In mid-November 1964, Shaikh Saqr bin Sultan al-Qasimi left Sharjah and went to Riyadh at the invitation of King Faisal bin 'Abdul-'Aziz, the King of Saudi Arabia. During the meeting, King Faisal talked about a project for the construction of a road that would be sponsored by the Kingdom of Saudi Arabia.

After Shaikh Saqr bin Sultan al-Qasimi returned from Riyadh, he consulted the British Political Agent in Dubai, H. Glen Balfour-Paul, about the issue of assistance provided by King Faisal of Saudi Arabia or the League of Arab States to finance development projects in the coastal emirates. Only a few days before the arrival of the Arab League Mission, Balfour-Paul had been appointed as the British Political Agent in Dubai. He would be replacing James Craig, who had taken the place of Balfour-Paul at the British Embassy in Beirut.

The response of Frank Brenchley, Head of the Arabian Department in the British Foreign Office, was as follows:

I recommend that in the discussion with Sir William Luce [the British Political Resident in the Gulf, whose headquarters were in Bahrain], the Ministry must provide suggested answers to the ruler of Sharjah through Mr Balfour-Paul. These should be endorsed in principle by Sir William Luce and should be as follows:

a) For the Saudis: The Government of Her Britannic Majesty welcomes in principle the granting of financial aid to the Roads

Fund which is managed by the Trucial States Council. In the next Council's meeting, the offer presented on this issue shall be a subject for discussion.

b) For the Arab League: The Trucial States Council will look in the near future into the best way of spending and management of any financial support for their development plans which the Arab League may consider putting forward.

On 17 December 1964, the Technical Mission for the League of Arab States arrived at Sharjah airport. There was a storm that day with very heavy rain. On their way from Sharjah airport to the Oasis Hotel in Dubai, the Mission saw the suffering that the people of the emirates had experienced. Their cars stopped a number of times when they became mired in the mud, and the car that was carrying their bags only made it to the hotel twenty-four hours after leaving Sharjah airport.

The Technical Mission of the League of Arab States was composed of:

- Dr Muhammad Salim – Head of Mission, from the United Arab Republic, President of the Federation of Industries
- 'Ali Fahmi al-Kashif – for water, from the United Arab Republic, Technical Director for the General Company for Research and Groundwater
- Isma'il Muhammad 'Abdul-'Al – for agriculture, from the United Arab Republic
- Ghaith Khair al-Din al-Zarkali – for public health, from the Kingdom of Saudi Arabia
- Muhammad Yusuf al-Rumi – for roads, from Kuwait

- Ahmad 'Azab Karim – for roads, from the United Arab Republic
- Muhammad 'Abdul-Ghani al-Khuli – for electricity, from the United Arab Republic
- 'Abdul-Hamid al-Bakir – for education, from Iraq
- Dr Ahmad Sa'id – for the economy, from the United Arab Republic
- Muhammad Sa'd al-Din – for trade, from the United Arab Republic

The next day, 18 December 1964, the Technical Mission of the League of Arab States visited Shaikh Saqr bin Sultan al-Qasimi and had dinner with him. Numerous dignitaries were invited. The British Political Agent in Dubai, Mr Balfour-Paul, was also invited. He wrote a letter to the British Political Resident in the Gulf, Sir William Luce, after talking to Dr Muhammad Salim, the Head of the Technical Mission, in the *majlis* of Shaikh Saqr bin Sultan al-Qasimi, following dinner that night. He wrote in the letter, 'I said to Dr Muhammad Salim, whom I know well from the Arab Petroleum Conference which was held in Beirut a short while ago, if the League of Arab States were serious about contributing to the development of the emirates, it is hoped that they would pay the money to the Central Development Fund, which is managed by the Trucial States Council. If not, there would be the risk of interference between the plans of the Council and our plans, apart from the plans of the Kuwait Office.'

Mr Balfour-Paul said in his letter to Sir William Luce that Muhammad Salim told him that the League of Arab States had different ideas. Their contribution would be managed by an agency similar to the Technical Assistance Fund of the United Nations. This meant that the Arab League could provide assistance directly to projects and emirates not necessarily through the Central Development Fund. He also mentioned that 'Abdul Khaliq Hassuna confirmed to him that a sum of six million pounds sterling would be requested in the meeting of Arab Prime Ministers in the League of Arab States, which would be held on 9 January 1965.

The Technical Mission spent four days travelling around the emirates. The most important thing the members of the Mission said, with great insistence, was the necessity for building a good road for periods of rain, as well as a survey of water resources and soil analysis.

On 27 January 1965, a meeting was held in Dubai between Shaikh Saqr bin Sultan al-Qasimi, the Ruler of Sharjah, and Mr Balfour-Paul, the British Political Agent. Mr Balfour-Paul had come from Bahrain two days earlier after a meeting with Sir William Luce, who had authorised him to talk without reservation to Shaikh Saqr, and to use any means or methods he saw fit to put political pressure on him and to bring him under control. The British were also very anxious to keep under control all political developments in the Gulf including the emerging relations between separate emirates and the Arab countries. The direct Arab League assistance to Sharjah and other emirates would weaken such control.

The last words of warning from Mr Balfour-Paul are contained in the following question:

'Has he been faithful or unfaithful to the Agreement signed with Her Majesty's Government when he assumed power, knowing its conditions? If he has been faithful, he should explain his behaviour; if he has been unfaithful, then he should not expect the Government of Her Britannic Majesty to remain silent.'

The response from Shaikh Saqr was that he did not have any funds to develop his underdeveloped country, and consequently he had to accept assistance from whoever offered it.

At the beginning of February 1965, the League of Arab States issued some resolutions providing for the following:

- The creation of a fund for the League which is funded through voluntary contributions from Arab countries including the emirates in the Gulf region. This is to be spent on assistance for the coastal emirates to provide services to them.
- Contributions could be in the form of the supply of technicians and experts as an alternative to financial contribution.
- Creation of a standing committee of the League of Arab States to consider the assistance given to the emirates and the management of that assistance. This would be under the leadership of the Secretary-General of the League, and members chosen from the participating states and emirates.
- The Secretary-General of the League of Arab States said that he would present the resolutions in the annual report to the kings and heads of state.

The Saudi delegation rejected these resolutions in a statement explaining the reasons why they could not agree to the Council's resolutions, emphasising that each of the emirates must agree to the resolutions in writing. This was also expressed by the Kuwaiti Minister Badr al-Khalid.

## *Arab/British rivalry in the Gulf*

Those gathered at the meeting of the League of Arab States decided to send Dr Sayyid Nufal, the Deputy Secretary-General of the League of Arab States, to the emirates to obtain the written agreement from each Ruler separately.

The British authorities in the Gulf rushed to set up an alternative fund to that established by the League of Arab States.

In the meeting that was held at the Trucial States Council on 1 March 1965, the Rulers decided to establish the Trucial States Development Office along with a trust fund. They also decided to invite all donors to send all development aid through that fund.

Shaikh Saqr, the Ruler of Sharjah, attracted the attention of those present with news from Beirut reporting that Sayyid Nufal, the Deputy Secretary-General of the Arab League, would arrive within a week along with financial assistance of an estimated million and a half pounds sterling. He was assured that the League of Arab States was keen on the participation of Rulers in the responsibility of the management of the fund.

The establishment of a common fund was desired by all parties, as all of the Rulers would have representatives in the office. Also, some professional experts would assist them in this work.

However, according to what was said by Badr al-Khalid, who became the personal representative of the Ruler of Kuwait in the Gulf Committee of the League of Arab States, which was established as a result of the Mission's 1964 report: 'The League of Arab States based in Cairo made a decision to provide assistance of five million pounds sterling within the next five years to the coastal emirates, and perhaps the League would write to the Rulers to ask for their agreement to this.'

On 10 May 1965, Dr Sayyid Nufal, the Deputy Secretary-General of the League of Arab States, arrived in Dubai. Twenty-four hours later, the British Minister of State at the Foreign Office, George Thomson, arrived.

Sayyid Nufal didn't waste any time. He claimed that a sum of £900,000 was at his disposal. He stated that there was a further £250,000 from Kuwait, and a similar amount from Iraq, as well as £400,000 from the United Arab Republic.

The following morning, 11 May 1965, Sayyid Nufal visited Shaikh Saqr bin Sultan al-Qasimi, the Ruler of Sharjah, in his *majlis* in Sharjah. After a lengthy discussion, he carried with him the following message for the Secretary-General of the Arab League:

In confirmation of the discussion which took place on this day between myself and Dr Sayyid Nufal, Deputy Secretary-General of the League of Arab States, I would like to express my gratitude to the League of Arab States for the development plans they have drawn up. I welcome the immediate start to their implementation. I would like also to express my gratitude for the arrangements made for the establishment of an office in the Emirate of Sharjah.

On the morning of 12 May 1965, Shaikh Saqr bin Sultan al-Qasimi went to Dubai to attend a meeting arranged by the British Political Agent in Dubai between the British Minister, George Thomson, and the Rulers of the coastal emirates. Each Ruler was to meet with him separately. The meetings were to be held in the British Agency in Dubai. The Ruler of Fujairah didn't attend as he had gone to undertake the Hajj pilgrimage.

The British Minister focused his discussion on topics which were of great importance to both the British Political Resident in the Gulf, Sir William Luce, and the British Political Agent in Dubai. These were as follows:

- Her Majesty's Government is determined to remain within the Gulf region, maintaining its agreements and obligations towards the Rulers.

- The increasing pressure and hostility to our position as well as the Rulers makes it necessary for the Rulers to cooperate with each other and with us. The Egyptians and Iraqis will exploit any differences to the detriment of all parties. Furthermore, Her Majesty's Government urges the Rulers to overcome their differences and bury them, and to find areas of cooperation with each other.

- In particular, the Rulers must stand together in support of the resolutions made by the Trucial States Council, as decided at the first meeting in March. They must insist that all external support come through the channel of the Emirates Development Fund.

In these meetings, the Ruler of Ras al-Khaimah, who was supposed to be meeting with Mr Nufal afterwards, was somewhat hesitant and frowning. The Ruler of Sharjah, who didn't say what he had agreed upon with Mr Nufal, seemed unhappy, and behaved in a rather stern manner.

That evening, Sayyid Nufal visited Shaikh Rashid bin Humaid al-Nu'aimi, the Ruler of 'Ajman, Shaikh Ahmad bin Rashid al-Mu'alla, the Ruler of Umm al-Qaiwain, and Shaikh Saqr bin Muhammad al-Qasimi, the Ruler of Ras al-Khaimah.

In the meeting with Shaikh Rashid bin Humaid al-Nu'aimi, the Ruler of 'Ajman, Sayyid Nufal urged the Shaikh to give him a letter similar to the letter of Shaikh Saqr bin Sultan al-Qasimi. However Shaikh Rashid bin Humaid al-Nu'aimi explained that the Rulers had agreed on establishing a fund for the Development Council, in which all donations to the emirates would be put.

At the insistence of Mr Nufal, the Ruler of 'Ajman gave him a letter similar to that of Shaikh Saqr bin Sultan al-Qasimi, with the exception of the last sentence regarding the opening of an office of the League of Arab States.

In the meeting between Sayyid Nufal and Shaikh Ahmad bin Rashid al-Mu'alla, the Ruler of Umm al-Qaiwain, he received the following letter, which was addressed to the Secretary-General of the League of Arab States:

I am pleased to send a message to Your Excellency welcoming the assistance which those in the Arab League have resolved to provide to us and our brethren in Coastal Oman. We thank Your Excellency for the sympathy and attention you provided for us, and we ask God to grant you and us success.

Shaikh Saqr bin Muhammad al-Qasimi, the Ruler of Ras al-Khaimah, wrote the following letter to the Secretary-General of the League of Arab States:

> Today we were visited by His Excellency Dr Nufal, and we are delighted with what he said to us. In confirmation of our discussion with him, I am pleased to inform Your Excellency that we welcome all of your efforts in helping this region within the Arab world. We declare our agreement with the possibility of opening an office of the League of Arab States in Ras al-Khaimah. We are therefore pleased to provide one of our new buildings in Oman Street as a modest gift to the League of Arab States. We hope that this will be suitable for the establishment of an office for the Arab League in our emirate.

## British anger with the Ruler of Sharjah

The British Minister of State accepted the invitation of Shaikh Saqr bin Sultan al-Qasimi, the Ruler of Sharjah, to have tea with him the following day, 13 May 1965. This was due to the Minister's decision to postpone the final confrontation with Shaikh Saqr until that time.

During the tea party hosted by Shaikh Saqr in the general *majlis* in his guest house in Sharjah, a meeting was held between Shaikh Saqr and the British Minister of State, George Thomson.

Attending the meeting alongside the British Minister were Sir William Luce, the British Political Resident in the Gulf, and Mr Balfour-Paul, the British Political Agent in Dubai, who translated between the Ruler and the British Minister.

Mr Thomson said, 'I have warned you previously about working with the Arab League. You informed me that you support this cooperation, and would agree to open an office of the League of Arab States in Sharjah. I want to talk to you again today about this matter, in a formal capacity. I want to ask you, did you give Dr Sayyid Nufal a letter agreeing to the plans of the Arab League?'

The Ruler replied, 'Yes. I gave him a letter of agreement to our cooperation with the Arab League, and that is final.'

Mr Thomson went on, 'The treaty concluded between you and the British prevents you from engaging in contact with any foreign party, with respect to external policy, except through the British Political Resident in the Gulf, or in your region. As you are also aware, our interests are your interests, and these interests must be maintained.'

The Ruler said, 'We are hungry and thirsty. The hungry accept assistance from any country that offers it.'

The Minister of State replied, 'This does not fall within the bounds of your authority.'

The Ruler said, 'The Mission of the Arab League came six months ago. Why didn't you oppose it at that time?'

Mr Thomson responded, 'We are concerned about your interests.'

The Ruler said, 'Are you concerned about *our* interests or *your* interests?'

Mr Thomson said, 'Let's get back to the subject at hand. Do you still insist on the position you expressed with regard to the Arab League?'

'The matter is final,' the Ruler replied.

Mr Thomson said, 'This is inconsistent with the treaty concluded with us.'

The Ruler said in response, 'I'm not the first to agree to cooperation with the Arab League. I ask that Britain not be content with looking at her immediate interests, but consider the future as well. Otherwise a problem will arise like that seen in Aden or Bahrain.'

Mr Thomson asked, 'Did you not agree that your rule would involve no contact with any foreign government before consulting the Political Resident?'

The Ruler replied, 'I pledged that my concern would be for the interests of my country above all else.'

Mr Thomson said, 'But you are bound to the treaty. The treaty states that Britain will manage all of your foreign policy.'

The Ruler replied, 'This treaty is unfair, as it was concluded between a strong party and a weak one, and so must be reconsidered.'

Mr Thomson said, 'We insist that an Arab League office not be opened in the region.'

The Ruler responded, 'There are offices for non-Arab countries in the region, and Kuwait has an office in the region.'

Mr Thomson said, 'The Kuwait Office is an old matter.' Then he added, 'I ask that you have a long think about this. It is a very dangerous matter.'

The Ruler said, 'At the moment, I am not thinking hard about any matters, whether dangerous or not: my concern is for the development of my country.'

Mr Thomson replied, 'You have agreed to the resolutions of the Trucial States Council and signed them, as agreed at the meeting on 1 March, that any support coming from outside must pass through the channel of the Trucial States Development Fund.'

The Ruler said, 'Consider this to be null and non-binding.'

That statement was followed by a period of silence, during which the British Minister looked around the room for a moment. Then he resumed the debate.

He said, 'You live in a beautiful home, with all its conveniences.'

The Ruler replied, 'I'm not interested in this house. I am really not that concerned as to whether it is beautiful or ugly. What I don't want is people cursing my children after I am gone.'

Mr Thomson said, 'We spend millions a year on a hundred thousand people in the emirates.'

The Ruler asked, 'Are you talking about what you pay the army and the Trucial Oman Scouts?'

The Minister replied, 'The Trucial Oman Scouts were established firstly for the protection of the Ruler, and secondly for the protection of the oil pipelines.'

The Ruler said, 'I have had nothing to thank the British government for over the years.'

The Foreign Minister responded, 'For the third time, I ask you to reconsider this matter. We do not want an office of the Arab League opened.'

The Ruler said, 'No. I cannot withdraw from the agreement. You can do whatever you want by force. I want to remind you that a British MP said recently in the British Parliament, "The emirates are independent, and responsible for their own actions. We are not responsible for their failure to develop."'

Mr Thomson said, 'I was the one who was speaking in Parliament. But I said that you are independent with regard to your internal affairs. Your foreign affairs and defence are control-led by Britain. I must insist that an office for the Arab League not be opened here.'

The Ruler replied, 'Neither I nor any Arab Ruler can prohibit the Arab League from coming to the coast, or stop their frater-nal assistance from reaching here, while you allow foreign aid to come here from yourselves and other non-Arab countries.'

The Foreign Minister said, 'You can borrow from any source, and you can accept help from Russia or China, or anywhere else. But we will not allow the opening of an office of the Arab League. We will prevent this from happening with all our might.'

The Ruler replied, 'Britain's friendship has become a stab in the back and a barrier to our progress. Besides, what makes Britain decide to open a development office then? If the reason is love, then why is this happening now? If the reason is fear, the Arabs are our brothers, and we will not reject their aid.'

The British Minister said, 'I thank you for your openness. But do not rush to open an office of the Arab League. I will raise your concerns with the Prime Minister.'

For more than a month, the British authorities used both carrots and sticks to try to change Shaikh Saqr bin Sultan al-Qasimi's mind on the matter of the League of Arab States. They tried to convince him to withdraw the letter delivered to Sayyid Nufal, the Assistant Secretary-General of the League of Arab States, or to convince him to send a new letter saying that he would accept the assistance of the Arab League to the emir-ates, provided that any contribution from the member states in the Arab League went to the Trucial States Development Fund.

However, Shaikh Saqr bin Sultan al-Qasimi had burnt all his bridges, and there was no turning back from his decision.

## Removal of Shaikh Saqr and the installation of my brother Shaikh Khalid

At ten o'clock on the morning of 24 June 1965, Shaikh Saqr bin Sultan al-Qasimi, the Ruler of Sharjah, left Sharjah Fort to go to the British Political Agency in Dubai. He was going to meet the British Political Agent, Mr Balfour-Paul, who had asked the Shaikh to visit him at the Agency.

On the way to Dubai, the procession of Shaikh Sultan al-Qasimi passed by the Nahda Hill. He didn't notice a group of workers collecting rubbish there. The group was composed of soldiers from the Oman Coast Force, whose mission was to inform the British Political Agency in Dubai that Shaikh Saqr bin Sultan al-Qasimi was passing by on his way to Dubai.

At the British Political Agency in Dubai, the British Political Agent, Mr Balfour-Paul, received Shaikh Saqr al-Qasimi and took him to his office. A moment later, two British officers entered the office of the Political Agent. One stood to the right of Shaikh Saqr and the other to his left. The Political Agent presented a signed document from individuals of the Qasimi family in Sharjah. The document stated their desire for Shaikh Saqr to step down and that Shaikh Khalid bin Muhammad al-Qasimi be recognised as the new Ruler of Sharjah.

Shaikh Saqr protested that the document was forged and the content was untrue. But Mr Balfour-Paul didn't give him the opportunity to finish what he wanted to say. He snapped, 'At the request of the new Ruler, Shaikh Khalid bin Muhammad al-Qasimi, the Ruler of Sharjah, I ask you to leave Sharjah immediately.'

Shaikh Saqr was led by the two British officers to the back door of the British Political Agency in Dubai, and put in a car, an Austin. He sat between the two British officers. The car was escorted by two Land Rovers which were carrying groups of men from the Oman Coast Force. The procession then headed to Sharjah airport. From the military section, he was put on a military aircraft of the British Royal Air Force and was flown to Bahrain.

Sharjah airport did not allow the next flight from Kuwait to land. On board that flight was the ousted Shaikh's son, Shaikh Sultan bin Saqr bin Sultan al-Qasimi, who had travelled to Cairo to join three of the professionals from the League of Arab States to Sharjah. Their mission was to establish the first office of the League of Arab States in Sharjah. It was decided that they would arrive at Sharjah airport on 24 November 1965, but the plane carrying the delegation was diverted from Sharjah to Doha, in Qatar. The delegation, along with Sultan bin Saqr al-Qasimi, was put down there.

In Sharjah, the Trucial Oman Scouts cordoned off the fort. They brought out 'Abdullah bin Sultan, the brother of Shaikh Saqr bin Sultan, and Khalid bin Saqr bin Muhammad al-Qasimi, the son of the Ruler of Ras al-Khaimah, who had rushed there after news spread of the removal of Shaikh Saqr bin Sultan al-Qasimi. The armed soldiers at the fort were also brought out from it.

At three o'clock that afternoon, Shaikh Khalid bin Muhammad al-Qasimi, the Ruler of Sharjah, under the protection of the

TOS, came from the TOS headquarters in Sharjah to the guest house, which was the general *majlis*, and was where Shaikh Khalid received well-wishers that evening.

On 25 June 1965, the following letter arrived:

From Sir William Luce, Political Resident to the Government of Her Majesty, Bahrain

To His Excellency, Shaikh Khalid bin Muhammad al-Qasimi, Ruler of Sharjah, Sharjah

Dear Sir,

I am authorised by the Government of Her Majesty the Queen of Britain to inform you that the Government officially recognises you as the Ruler of Sharjah, and on its part will fulfil all obligations to you as Ruler under the agreements concluded between the Government and your forebears among the Rulers of Sharjah.

This recognition has been granted on the understanding that you will accept in full your part in the obligations with respect to the agreements, treaties, transactions, and customs, which your forebears from among Rulers of Sharjah made with the Government of Her Britannic Majesty.

I would be grateful for a reply to this letter and its contents. Your letter along with mine would constitute official documents in recognition of your capacity as the Ruler of Sharjah by the Government of Her Britannic Majesty.

[The usual ending]

Signed: Sir William Luce

On 26 June 1965, Shaikh Khalid sent the following letter:

From Shaikh Khalid bin Muhammad al-Qasimi, Ruler of
Sharjah
   To His Excellency, Sir William Luce, Political Resident of
Her Britannic Majesty's Government

Dear Sir,
   I am honoured by your letter regarding the official recognition by Her Majesty of my accession to the throne and the
leadership of the Government of Sharjah and its subsidiaries.
   On this occasion, Your Excellency, I extend my sincere
appreciation to the Government of Her Britannic Majesty. I
assure you that I will abide by all pledges, commitments, agreements, treaties, transactions, and customs, which were held by
my predecessors among the Rulers of Sharjah.
   Similarly, I will keep and preserve completely the traditional
legacy of friendship that binds us. You can rest assured that I
will be worthy of your confidence.
   [The usual ending]
   Signed: Khalid bin Muhammad al-Qasimi,
   Ruler of Sharjah and its subsidiaries

## Chairman of the Municipality

At the time of the coup, which was carried out by Shaikh Khalid
bin Muhammad al-Qasimi, I was meeting with the management
of one of the Dubai sports clubs to arrange a football match.
I was the president of the Najah Club. This had replaced the

earlier People's Sports and Cultural Club, which had been shut down after the performance of my play *Zionist Agents*.

The Najah Club remained for years without a home base, so I rented a house in a traditional neighbourhood and we held our activities there. The news reached us at noon that Shaikh Saqr bin Sultan al-Qasimi had been removed from power by the British. I went back to our house, where I found out what had happened.

That afternoon, while I was on my way back to the club, I glimpsed rows of soldiers from the TOS in front of the court-yard of the fort and the guest house. But I didn't pay any attention to it.

In front of the Najah Club, there was some open ground where we had set up a volleyball net, and as usual we played volleyball while the people of the neighbourhood surrounded the court on all four sides to watch. Then a representative of Shaikh Khalid bin Muhammad al-Qasimi, the new Ruler of Sharjah – and my brother – came and asked me to go to the Shaikh. I told him that I would go by myself later.

After the sunset prayer, I went to the fort to find my brother, Shaikh Khalid bin Muhammad al-Qasimi, sitting with a group of men. I greeted him, and he noticed a look of unhappiness on my face. He took me aside and said, 'We didn't tell you because we knew what you would think.'

I replied, 'Come by any means except by means of the British.'

He said, 'Should I wait until he kills me? You yourself were a witness to this possibility when you were shot at.'

My brother was referring to an incident a week or so before the coup, when Shaikh Khalid bin Muhammad al-Qasimi had taken his wife to the Kuwait Hospital in Dubai. My mother asked me to take her there to visit her daughter-in-law. In front of the door of the hospital, I met my brother, Shaikh Khalid. I told him that when I returned to our house that night I had been fired upon from the roof of the garage at the fort.

Shaikh Khalid said, 'The shooting was aimed at me, and not you. That's why I got out of Sharjah, and it will only be a matter of time before you will be forced out.'

I said, 'Nobody can take me away from Sharjah.'

He muttered words from which I knew he was plotting something.

I said, 'Be wise, Khalid. Don't let your children end up orphans.'

Those were the last words uttered between us before the coup.

My brother Khalid said, 'What are you thinking about?'

I replied, 'I am thinking about what I said to you in front of the Kuwait Hospital in Dubai.'

Shaikh Khalid continued, 'I want you to be with me. You can take up any position you wish.'

'I can't,' I replied, 'because I'll be going to Cairo to study.'

'Even if only temporarily.'

'The Municipality,' I said.

'Agreed,' he replied.

I took up the position of Chairman of the Municipality, and I made Shaikh Su'ud bin Sultan al-Qasimi the Deputy Chairman. I was only able to stay in that position for two months, after which I asked my brother, the Ruler of Sharjah, to appoint Shaikh Su'ud bin Sultan to take over as Chairman of the Municipality.

I devoted my time to studying mathematics in preparation for the resitting of a final examination. My earlier result was invalidated because one of my classmates tried to cheat from my paper. I travelled to Kuwait and successfully resat the mathematics exam. I told the Ministry of Education to quickly send my papers to Egypt, and then I followed the papers there.

12

*University Years: Part 1*

I ARRIVED IN CAIRO AT THE end of September 1965, before the the academic year started at the beginning of October. My goal was to secure a place at the Faculty of Agriculture at Cairo University. A month and a half later, I was accepted.

## Helpful coincidences

One of the students was Omani. His name was Mahmoud 'Abdul-Nabi. He was studying in the Faculty of Agriculture and he knew the Director of Student Affairs, Mr Husain Jad. One morning Husain Jad said to Mahmoud 'Abdul-Nabi, 'Today another one of your countrymen has been accepted into the college.'

Mahmoud asked Husain Jad to tell him the name of the student, and he replied, after looking through some papers, 'Sultan bin Muhammad al-Qasimi' (I had written in my passport that my country was 'Oman' instead of 'the Emirate of Sharjah').

Mahmoud 'Abdul-Nabi walked out of the Faculty of Agriculture and went to the Sharjah students' residence. He obtained my address, which was near the Sharjah students' residence, and told me that I had been accepted into the Faculty of Agriculture at Cairo University, which is what I had been hoping for.

I went with Mahmoud 'Abdul-Nabi to the Faculty of Agriculture, where Mr Husain Jad took me through the steps I needed to follow to enrol at the college. He told me that I had to provide them with three passport photographs and a medical report. So I went immediately from the college to enquire about the fastest way to obtain the passport photographs. I was told that I would be able to have these done in front of the government department's compound at Tahrir Square in the centre of Cairo, so I went there and I had three photographs taken. However, the camera was very old, and the photographs it produced did not look at all like me. From Tahrir Square I went to the medical centre in Giza, where I was to have my physical examination, and then I was sent to another place to have my eyes examined. Once that was done, I was sent to yet another place where I was to have my X-ray. However, when I got there the place was crowded with a large number of students. Then the doctor in charge came to us and announced that the X-ray films had run out. He advised us to come back the following day. Everybody shuffled out of the door, but I stayed behind looking at the doctor. The doctor asked me, 'You, what do you want?'

I replied, 'I am a special case, and I have to get my residence permit tomorrow otherwise I will have pay a fine of fifty pounds for the delay. Residence is not granted until after one has obtained a card from the college, and to get the card from the college I must have the X-ray film. I am prepared to buy it from anywhere I can.'

The doctor interrupted me and said, 'We have a film for you.'

The doctor took me over to the X-ray room and instructed that I be given an X-ray. He advised me to return for the films in the morning. The next morning, I took the X-ray films and medical results and submitted them to the registration office. They accepted all of my papers except for the pictures which did not resemble me. Husain Jad intervened, promising that I would bring in some 'clean' pictures – as he described them – as soon as possible, and that the pictures I had already submitted would be used temporarily.

The whole process of my registration at the Faculty of Agriculture was completed within just twenty-four hours. Thus, a longer wait was avoided whereby the Faculty of Agriculture would first write to the Coordinating Bureau in Cairo, who would send a letter to the Ministry of Higher Education in Egypt, who in turn would contact the Embassy of Kuwait in Cairo. Then the Embassy would forward the matter to the Ministry of Education in Kuwait, and from there to the Kuwait Office in Dubai, who would contact me in Sharjah to inform me of my acceptance into the Faculty of Agriculture at Cairo University. I found out later that the Kuwait Office in Dubai had indeed contacted officials in Sharjah, who told them of my acceptance at the Faculty of Agriculture at Cairo University. This was more than an entire month after I had been accepted at the Faculty of Agriculture for the academic year 1965–66.

So began my first year of study at the Faculty of Agriculture, Cairo University.

## The Arab Club

In the summer holidays in mid-June 1966 I returned to Sharjah to find that the construction of the headquarters for the Arab Club had been completed. The only thing that remained incomplete was the amenities, so I put them in, and the club was opened. From this club I started publishing the magazine *Al-Yaqza* (Awareness), which was issued weekly and was printed at the print shop of Khalifa al-Nabudah in Dubai. The magazine continued for as long as I remained in Sharjah but ceased when I returned to Cairo to begin my second year at the Faculty of Agriculture. That was in September, at the beginning of the 1966–67 academic year.

In the second year of my studies, I took a course called 'Livestock Science'. The term 'livestock' referred to camels, cows, sheep and goats. The course was taught by Professor 'Abdul-Latif Badruddin, former Dean of the Faculty of Agriculture, who had a very good relationship with his students. Once he told us about something that happened during his doctoral studies at the Institute for Animal Husbandry at the University of Edinburgh in Scotland:

'The British Governor General in the Sudan sent a letter to the Director of the Institute for Animal Husbandry at the University of Edinburgh, asking him about how to improve the cattle in the Sudan. The Director immediately conveyed the request to his graduate students at the Institute, asking them to write him reports on how cattle in the Sudan could be improved.

'When the reports were handed in, the Director of the Institute just put them aside and did nothing with them. When the students protested about this, the Director replied that the reports would do nothing to help improve cattle in the Sudan and told his secretary to write this letter:

To the British Governor General of the Sudan,
    If you want to improve the cattle in the Sudan, improve the conditions of the people in the country first.'

## *The Presidential Palace*

The student unions at the University of Cairo, which were like students' clubs, were active from the beginning of the academic year; that was when the elections to the committees of the unions began. A surprising thing happened that year. Suddenly, and without warning, most of the student unions fell into the hands of the Arab Nationalist students. They celebrated in a triumphant way, provoking the unionists and the communists. The unionists tried to keep their activities going even after they had lost all their positions in the elections. They seized the opportunity to do this on the anniversary of the death of the martyr Majdali, who was from southern Arabia and had fought against the British in Aden. In order to turn that occasion into an event and attract attention, they organised a march through the streets of Cairo. However, the Egyptian authorities refused them permission, so it was decided that Mahmoud 'Abdul-Nabi and I among the Omani students would go to meet President Jamal Abdel Nasser.

After securing an appointment to meet the President, we went in the morning to the Presidential Palace. An officer met us at the gate and took us into the hall near the entrance. After just a moment, a car came from the Palace building with a person in civilian clothing inside. We didn't know his position or rank, but the guards all the way from the Palace building were saluting him.

In the Presidential Palace, we were received by Mr Nabil Fath al-Bab. He sat us in the hall near his office, after he took our request. After a long wait, he came to us to tell us, 'The President is very busy. He said that you may hold a commemoration, but you must not go out onto the streets.'

At the journalists' syndicate, in Gumhuriyya (Republic) Street, a commemoration was held. Among the speakers was Amin Jad'an, who had lost the presidency of the Association of Syrian Students and poured vitriol on the other side, that is, the nationalists. Then the arguments began, and after that a confrontation, and then a fight in which chairs on the stage of the syndicate were thrown around. The glass of the front window was smashed, and everyone went outside onto Gumhuriyya Street. The nationalists fled, and the unionists chased after them. The traffic came to a halt, and pedestrians gathered to watch on the pavements, which is just what the unionists wanted.

## *The bicycle*

Abu Qasidah was a student from the Dhofar region of Oman, and was studying in Cairo. He had arrived in Cairo with someone from Salalah who had been imprisoned for a few days back there. He had been riding a bicycle in the crowded Salalah Market, where riding bicycles is prohibited, and had bumped into one of the people. Abu Qasidah and his friend established the Dhofar Liberation Front. One day when some of us were walking along one of the streets in Cairo, we saw a sign hanging over the first floor of one of the buildings that caught our eyes. It read: Office of the Dhofar Liberation Front.

We went to have a closer look at the office. There was the man whose tale had been one of no more than riding a bicycle in the Salalah Market, for which he had been imprisoned for a few days. He had turned the story of the bicycle into a struggle, and the struggle into a revolution.

We contacted Mr Fathi al-Dib, a member of the Secretariat of the Socialist Union, the ruling party in Egypt, who was in fact the officer in charge of 'liberation movements in the Arab world'. We explained to him what that man was up to, and that Dhofar was a part of Oman. The Egyptian authorities closed the office immediately.

After a few days, the office was reopened and we realised that Abu Qasidah and the Arab Nationalists were behind the opening of the office the second time.

The issue of a bicycle had turned into an issue of a nation and a people!

## *The June 1967 War*

At the beginning of June 1967, preparations for war were being made. At the same time, the second semester exams of the second year in the Faculty of Agriculture had commenced.

We had already sat exams for a few courses when we heard the loud sounds of firing cannons. That was at noon on 5 June 1967. I went out onto the street and saw the people cheering and chanting *'Allahu Akbar'*. Others were peering up at the sky, trying to catch a glimpse of the warplanes as they flew high overhead on that dusty day.

I went to the 'Aguza neighbourhood, to the house of Yusuf al-Hasan and Riyad Abu Mahmoud, who was my colleague at the Faculty of Agriculture. From there we went to the Socialist Union building to meet Mr Fathi al-Dib.

There students from every Arab country had gathered. It was decided that we would join the volunteers who were requesting that they be taken to the front. We had not undergone any military training before, and so it was decided that we would be taken to the Bani Yusuf training camp at the area around the Pyramids. For two days we were given weapons training. Then came the order for us to be transferred to the military camp at the Al-Gazira Club.

We underwent two more days of training. Then, suddenly, on the night of 9 June 1967, President Jamal Abdel Nasser resigned!

Masses of people poured into the streets. The sun disappeared on that day, and we entered darkness, as all the street lights were turned off. I couldn't go anywhere because of the crowds of people filling the streets, so I sat on a wooden bench on the pavement of Al-Gazira Street, just past the Gala' Bridge, watching the people shuffle past me. I was overcome by emotion, which inspired me to make up a poem:

*My country, you hold a strange secret*
*The owner of the house in you is a stranger*
*Who is the one who mixed your dawn with your sunset?*
*Who melted your laughter into your weeping?*
*He is too close to me, to you and every friend*
*He is an enemy who takes out his arrows today*
*O regret, my country, O regret*
*The young girls in the innocence of childhood*
*And the young woman walking in shyness*
*And the boys in full manhood*
*And the youth, how he holds back his desires*
*And the old man didn't care when he grew old*
*All of them were robbed of the smile*
*O regret, my country, O regret*
*In my country the spider weaves its web*
*And there is division between the houses*
*There is a sick person in bed and another dies*
*And a paralysed person gets food for the children*
*A date, and bread and fish*
*And people laugh without censure*
*O regret, my country, O regret*
*My brother, let us rise and erase the damage*
*O brother, don't say this is fate!*
*With hope and effort we will achieve victory*
*With serenity and sincerity we will reach our goals*
*With faith, God had granted victory*
*O brother, let us protect our dignity*
*With courage O my country, with courage.*

The university exams resumed but I didn't pass some of the courses because of my psychological state at the time. After that, I travelled to Sharjah and found out that many things had been happening in my absence.

On 7 June 1967, people from all of the different emirates came and gathered at the Kuwait Office in Dubai. They demanded to be taken to Kuwait to serve as volunteers in the Egyptian army. Captain 'Abdul-Aziz bin Muhammad al-Qasimi and Captain Faisal bin Sultan al-Qasimi resigned from the Trucial Oman Scouts and were among those demanding to volunteer for the Egyptian forces. The people gathered for four days, shouting, cursing the British and the Americans, but to no avail. The doors of the Kuwait Office didn't open to take the crowds to Kuwait.

In Sharjah, on the evening of 7 June 1967, a fire broke out at the Sailing Club in Al-Hira which belonged to the Trucial Oman Scouts and the British Royal Air Force. The fire gutted the building, which was built of palm branches. Some boats were also burnt before a fire engine belonging to the Air Force could get to it to put it out. As soon as the fire engine arrived, the gathering crowds began pelting it with stones so that the men inside were forced to turn the hose on the crowds instead of the fire.

On 8 June, it was discovered that the wires between the Voice of the Coast radio station and the radio transmitter had been cut, and it stopped broadcasting for an entire day. The station had been set up by the British at their base in Sharjah, and it broadcast in Arabic.

## *A visit to Karachi*

I couldn't stand hearing the news in Sharjah, which was passed on by word of mouth, hour by hour, about the war and its progress. So I decided to travel to Pakistan, to the city of Karachi.

I spent ten days in Karachi. I saw the important sites in the city, which were few in number. The most important landmark is the Defence Mosque, which is shaped like a large dome with no pillars. It accommodates thousands of worshippers. However, there weren't many worshippers at the mosque for the sunset prayer. That mosque was in the most prestigious district of Karachi, the 'Defence' quarter, built on high ground in the east of the city. The streets were clean there, and it had attractive houses surrounded by gardens, with flowering trees overhanging their walls.

The following evening, I went to the poorest neighbourhood in Karachi, called Lyari. This neighbourhood is in the west of the city, and spreads over several kilometres. I wandered through the streets, and saw that the houses were huts built from sheets of tin and the streets were overflowing with foul-smelling sewage.

## *Lazoghli: Encounter with Egyptian State Security*

After Karachi, I visited Sharjah for a few days, then returned to Cairo to complete my studies in the remaining subjects of the second year (1967–68) at the Faculty of Agriculture. My brother, Shaikh Khalid bin Muhammad al-Qasimi, sent me a white Mercedes, a 1968 model, which had just come onto the market.

I had only a small number of courses remaining, so I invested my time in studying the Islamic inscriptions on the mosques and historical buildings. My car used to draw people's attention when I stopped in front of the mosques and buildings. A young man (me) would get out to examine the buildings carefully and then get back into the car. Sometimes he would climb onto a pile of rubble that covered a part of the building. The intelligence officers who had been assigned to watch me got very tired, as my car was much faster than theirs. This forced the Department of Security to give Major Shaukat Husni the task of contacting me. He was employed to monitor the activities of Arab students. I had met him several times on various occasions, but we had previously only greeted each other.

'I want to get to know you!' he told me.

I said, 'On one condition. That you remove the shadow that is following me around!'

'This matter is controlled by the "big man",' he said.

'Who?!' I asked. 'Abdel Nasser?!'

'No. Our man in Lazoghli.'

'Where?' I asked.

'In the Department of Security.'

Major Shaukat Husni arranged for me to meet General Mahmoud Sha'rawi, the Chief of the Division of Arab Activities. He was very polite when we met. He asked for one of the employees to come in. When the employee arrived, the general said, 'Give me Sultan's file.'

'Do you have a file on me?' I asked.

'Of course,' he replied. 'Everyone has a file.'

In the twinkling of an eye, the file was brought in. It was as if it had already been brought out for that meeting. General Mahmoud Sha'rawi opened the file and turned the pages as he read it. He said, 'On that day you visited that place.'

He started counting the places that I had visited, and asked, 'What were you doing there?'

I replied, 'I was getting to know Egypt.'

Then he asked, 'Getting to know Egypt in these places?'

I replied, 'Do you want me to get to know Egypt in Haram Street?!' (Haram Street is filled with nightclubs.)

'Heavens no!' he said.

He stood up to say goodbye, leaving the file open on the desk.

I asked him, 'Are you going to leave this file open?'

He went over to close the file, and said, 'We will close it!'

I asked, 'Will you close it in the other sense too?'

He replied, 'We will close it in the other sense too.'

## My brother 'Abdul-'Aziz, the Deputy Governor of Khor Fakkan

I passed the remaining courses for the second year of my studies, and then returned to Sharjah in mid-June 1968 to find that a dispute had erupted between my three brothers.

Shaikh Saqr, the Deputy Ruler, had distanced himself from his brother, Shaikh Khalid bin Muhammad al-Qasimi, the Ruler of Sharjah. This was because of his inability to get along with Mr Jasim bin Saif al-Midfa', Secretary to the Ruler.

Shaikh Khalid, the Ruler, intended to establish a police force in Sharjah. After consulting the British Political Agent in Dubai, the Political Resident welcomed the idea. Shaikh Khaled's brother, Shaikh 'Abdul-'Aziz, had remained without a job up to this time so he gave a mandate to 'Abdul-'Aziz to establish the police force. The British Political Agent opposed this idea, saying that the establishment of the police required a specialist in that field. The British quickly put forward Mr Burns, who was British.

Shaikh Khalid went back and told the British Political Agent that he would appoint Shaikh 'Abdul-'Aziz to be the Chief of Police, and Mr Burns would be under the authority of 'Abdul-'Aziz. The British Political Agent opposed this, and told Shaikh Khalid that Burns would take orders only from Shaikh Khalid, the Ruler of Sharjah, and nobody else, and that there was no need to appoint 'Abdul-'Aziz.

So, at the beginning of May 1968, Shaikh Khalid bin Muhammad al-Qasimi appointed Shaikh 'Abdul-'Aziz bin Muhammad al-Qasimi as Deputy Ruler in the Sharqiyya (Eastern) region, the base of which was in Khor Fakkan. He was appointed in place of 'Uthman Barut, who was transferred to a lower ranking post than his previous one.

After Shaikh 'Abdul-'Aziz had assumed his new position, an argument broke out in the market at Khor Fakkan between an Indian barber and a Sharjah citizen concerning the price of mangoes being sold by an Indian fruitseller. The argument turned into a fist fight between the two men. Because the barber was holding his scissors in one hand, he injured the local man who called to the other citizens at the market for help. A small fight broke out, with the Indians and Pakistanis who were looking after the shops on the one side, and the local people who were in the market on the other. Some of the shops were damaged. 'Abdul-'Aziz arrested twenty-eight locals from Khor Fakkan who were in the market, with a group of police he had put together himself, like the core of a police squad. The local citizens were put in jail. As soon as the news reached Shaikh Khalid, he ordered that they all be released.

Shaikh 'Abdul-'Aziz claimed that Shaikh Khalid had ruined his prestige and authority in the Sharqiyya region, and that 'Uthman Barut had maliciously spread news of events in Khor Fakkan to Shaikh Khalid in Sharjah in the hope that he would be moved to intervene.

## Offer of the post of Deputy Ruler of Sharjah

Shaikh Khalid, the Ruler of Sharjah, asked me to present myself as his Deputy whenever he was absent due to travelling to England. I asked him to make it up with his brother, Shaikh Saqr, before he travelled. He agreed to this.

I contacted Saqr and presented the matter to him. He refused to go to the Shaikh, commenting, 'He should come to me.' I suggested that he could come to the living room in the private area of the Palace, and that Shaikh Khalid would come to us there. He agreed to that arrangement.

We were sitting in the living room when Shaikh Khalid came in. Shaikh Saqr shook hands with his brother, Shaikh Khalid. Shaikh Khalid talked about issues that were not related to the one we were dealing with. I went up to Shaikh Khalid and said, 'Allow me, Your Highness. You instructed me to represent you, and that was at the time of the disagreement between you and

Saqr. Now, praise be to Allah, there is no longer a disagreement to your meeting. Do you, Shaikh Saqr, have any objection to this?'

Shaikh Saqr responded, 'No. I have no objection. You and I are one and the same.'

When we were about to leave, Shaikh Khalid asked, 'Shall we all have lunch together?'

I replied, 'Brother Saqr has invited me to have lunch with him.'

Shaikh Khalid, the Ruler of Sharjah, decided to travel to Britain the first week of July 1968. There was a large crowd to bid him farewell at Dubai airport. Shaikh 'Abdul-'Aziz arrived late, and before the aircraft door was closed, he rushed into the plane. There he said goodbye to Shaikh Khalid. He asked, 'Do you have any instructions for me, Your Highness?'

Shaikh Khalid replied, 'As I told you previously, you are responsible for the government in the Sharqiyya region, and nothing else.'

Shaikh 'Abdul-'Aziz asked, 'What should I do if a disturbance breaks out in Sharjah?'

Shaikh Khalid replied, 'Sultan bin Muhammad will deal with it.'

Shaikh Khalid was away from Sharjah for six weeks, which he spent in London. In Sharjah during that time a strange incident took place. Armed Bedouin had surrounded the Agriculture Office in Maliha. I had to drive a Land Rover, taking some policemen with me, through the burning summer sands to the Maliha region, which was forty kilometres from the city of Sharjah.

When I arrived in Maliha, I spoke to the leader of the Bedouin, 'Awadh bin Saif al-Khasuni. He told me that a Pakistani man was hiding in the Agriculture Office with a British gentleman, the Director of the Agriculture Office. The Pakistani had sexually interfered with a camel, and so the British man should hand him over.

I convinced 'Awadh bin Saif that I would take the Pakistani to Sharjah to deal with his punishment, and that he, 'Awadh bin Saif, could come with me to see for himself that the punishment had been administered.

With a group of policemen who were with me, the Pakistani was handed over by the Director of the Agriculture Office. I put him with the police in the car I had come in. 'Awadh bin Saif sat with me in the car until we arrived in Sharjah. I ordered that the Pakistani be taken to the court. The judge at the court was Shaikh Muhammad al-Tandi, who was Egyptian. I advised him to inform me of the sentence before it was implemented.

While I was waiting for the news of the sentence passed on the Pakistani, the telephone rang. It was the Assistant British Political Agent, Mr Terence J. Clark, who was acting on behalf of the British Political Agent, David Roberts (whose period of service in the emirates had ended), while waiting for the new appointee to the position, who had not yet arrived.

After he had greeted me, the Assistant Political Agent said, 'Shaikh Sultan, the Indians and Pakistanis are under the protection of the British. They cannot be punished through the local courts. They can only be punished through the British Political Agency.'

I said, 'The Pakistani has committed a despicable act. He should be punished by Islamic law, as he is a Muslim.'

The Assistant Agent said, 'We will prosecute him. You don't know the agreements between the British and the Shaikhs of the emirates.'

I replied, 'I have no objection, but only when the British Agency has its own Islamic court . . .'

The phone rang again. It was Shaikh Muhammad al-Tandi. He said, 'The sentence is one hundred lashes!'

I said, 'Carry out the punishment!'

The next morning, I saw a convoy of tanks moving into 'Uruba Street, from north to south of the city of Sharjah. I called Mr Clark and said, 'These tanks that are moving through Sharjah. Is this a threat directed at me?'

Mr Clark replied, 'No. I know nothing about this!'

I said, 'By God, if this provocation isn't stopped, I will bring the whole town out to pelt those tanks with stones.'

Mr Clark replied, 'Don't give us trouble. I am coming to see you now.'

Half an hour later, Mr Clark, the British Assistant Political Agent, arrived. I received him in my office at the guest house, where most of the government departments were located. Our conversation went as follows:

I said, 'If I had not done what I did in Meleiha, the Pakistani and the British man would have been killed. Instead of that, one hundred lashes were given, after which the Pakistani simply shook his shirt out and walked.'

Mr Clark said, 'Thank you for this action.'

I replied, 'You thank me for this by sending tanks into the main street in the centre of the city?!'

Mr Clark said, 'I have no knowledge of those tanks. When I asked about them, I was told that the tanks belonged to the

British forces. They were let out in the Hira neighbourhood in Sharjah, and were heading to the British base.'

I replied, 'Sorry for what I said this morning.'

Mr Clark said, 'That's alright. But I ask you to consider me a friend. Refer to me if there are any problems that might be hard for you to deal with.'

'Let's remain friends,' I said.

Mr Clark said, 'Tonight the new British Political Agent, Mr Julian Bullard, is arriving at Dubai airport from Britain. I want you to come with me to meet him.'

I replied, 'I will be there before the plane lands.'

When the plane landed, Mr Clark shook hands with the new British Political Agent and introduced me to him. He said, 'This is Shaikh Sultan bin Muhammad al-Qasimi, brother of the Ruler of Sharjah, and Deputy Ruler of Sharjah, although he has been receiving education from the Egyptians.'

When we were on our way to the VIP suite, I introduced myself. I said, 'I was born in Sharjah and educated here. I studied in the schools here and worked as a teacher at the Trade School of the British Political Agency for three years. I went to Egypt recently to complete my university studies.'

Shaikh Khalid bin Muhammad al-Qasimi came back from London to Sharjah, and before I asked him for permission to travel to Egypt to complete my studies there, Yusri al-Duwaik, Shaikh Khalid's legal adviser, asked to see me about an important matter.

When we met, he offered me the post of Deputy Governor of the Sharqiyya region, taking the place of Shaikh 'Abdul-'Aziz. I rejected the offer, giving the excuse that I had to continue my studies.

The next day, Yusri al-Duwaik offered me a different position, that of Deputy Ruler of Sharjah. He said, 'The matter doesn't require a new decree, as you are still the Deputy Ruler.'

I asked, 'What happened to Shaikh Saqr and Shaikh 'Abdul-'Aziz for me to take their positions?'

He replied, 'The relationship between them has soured, leaving only you. You are the only one left.'

I said, 'I will have to decline. I am leaving for Cairo now.'

The following morning, I bade Shaikh Khalid farewell, without discussing the subject of the new position.

13

*University Years: Part* 2

IN SEPTEMBER 1968, I ARRIVED in Cairo to begin the first semester of my third year at the Faculty of Agriculture.

My brother, Shaikh Saqr bin Muhammad al-Qasimi, visited me at my house in Cairo in the month of Ramadan that year. He came directly from the airport, and he was grumbling. I greeted him and asked, 'What's the matter?'

He replied, 'What kind of a country is this where we are met by cemeteries and foul odours everywhere?'

I knew now why he was grumbling. The taxi driver had come from the airport via Salah Salim Road, were there is a cemetery. Then it went past Majra al-'Uyun, where there is a tannery that emits foul smells.

I said, 'After you have had a rest, I will take you to have a look around Cairo.'

I took him into Cairo from the direction of the airport. After that, we returned via Al-'Uruba Street, and from there we went to Heliopolis, where the buildings were elegant and the modern streets had recently been planted with trees. Then we went back home to break our Ramadan fast at sunset.

After breaking our fast, I told him that I would take him to the Al-Husain area to pray the special Ramadan *tarawih* prayer at Al-Husain Mosque. The squares and main roads there were teeming with people waiting to offer the usual night prayer, which would be followed by the longer *tarawih* prayer. After the prayers had finished, the crowds of people dispersed like locusts swarming across the fields. There was a book sale in that area, as well as a temporary theatre where local singing and dancing bands performed their arts. Zakariya al-Hijjawi, a famous singer at that time, had returned from the country-side and was presenting a female singer named Khadra, and the Al-Buhaira group, which played the drums and performed their dance.

Just a few days later, Shaikh Saqr's earlier memories of the cemetery had been erased by all the beautiful historical buildings of Cairo. The foul smells of the tannery were no longer in his thoughts. In their place were the fragrant scents of Cairo's parks and gardens.

I sat the examination for the first semester of the third academic year. I passed all of the courses, and moved up to the second semester of the third year.

At that time, 'Umair bin 'Abdullah al-Flasi, a merchant from Dubai and a friend, visited Cairo and stayed at the Omar Khayyam Hotel. As it was so crowded in the hotels around Cairo at that time, the hotel owners had built extra rooms out of wood in the hotel garden. 'Umair bin 'Abdullah was one of the guests staying in those extra rooms. The wooden walls of these rooms were so thin that all the loud noises outside could be heard in the rooms.

When I visited Mr 'Umair in his room, he complained to me about the banging of the drums, the dancing and the singing that took place every night. He invited me to dinner, and took me to the main building in the hotel where there was a restaurant. When we got to the hotel lobby, there was a wedding reception with the deafening sounds of drums and flutes as the bride was coming down the stairs. A dancer, with very little clothing covering her body, was leading the way. All of a sudden, she was right in front of us. We wanted to get away, but we were hemmed in by the crowd of well-wishers behind us. We couldn't find an escape, so one of us was to the right of the bride and the other to the left of the groom, until the party finished.

Mr 'Umair bin 'Abdullah asked me after that, 'Is this allowed?!'

I said, 'Will you say the Friday prayer with me tomorrow?'

'Yes!' he replied.

Before the Friday prayer, I accompanied 'Umair bin 'Abdullah to Qasr al-Nil (Nile Palace) Street, where the Casablanca Café, owned by Muhammad 'Abdul-Salam, was located. I had with me two prayer rugs that I had asked him to bring for me that morning.

We set off for the Sharif Mosque in Sharif Street for our prayers, but the mosque was so full that people were praying outside in the street. We spread our rugs out on the ground and joined the last rows of worshippers. At that time, the congregation were repeating 'Amen . . . Amen . . . Amen . . . Amen!' to the Imam's supplications towards the end of the sermon.

'Umair bin Abdullah asked me, 'Where is the mosque?'
'Far away,' I replied.

He said, 'How great is the number of your believers, O Egypt!'

## The Omani Students' Association

The Omani Students' Association, which was located in Gumhuriyya Street, didn't have any students connected to the Arab Nationalist movement except for Abu Qasida, an Omani student from the Dhofar region. During the elections which were held at the Association, he had no one to vote for him but himself. So he started recruiting groups of Omani and Zanzibari students who were studying in Egyptian schools at the primary and secondary levels to join the Association. They received a small amount of assistance from the Egyptian Endowment Fund. The arrangements for their membership of the Omani Students' Association were made on the condition that they could not participate in the elections. Every student from Sharjah who had received study assistance from Kuwait had to pay the Association three Egyptian pounds every month. This was to be distributed by the Association to the non-university students who had newly joined the Association.

Abu Qasida couldn't find a way to gain control of the Association until a full year after the entry of the non-university students. Arrangements for a tea party were made, which was to be attended by a large number of both university and non-university students. At that time, I was the President of the

Association, and Rashid bin Sultan al-Makhawi was Treasurer. While we were enjoying ourselves at the gathering, one of the non-university students came up to me and threw a plate of fruit and cakes at my feet, exclaiming, 'We are not beggars! We do not need your charity!' He wanted to disrupt the event and provoke a fight to try to gain control of the Association.

I replied, 'There is no need to talk like that. This behaviour is unacceptable!'

He pushed me back and some of the university students stood by to defend me. Then a fight erupted involving all of the students. Eventually, the non-university students were defeated. They rushed down the stairs from the sixth floor with everyone following them, punching and kicking them, until they went out onto Gumhuriyya Street. We followed them some of the way, and then came back.

After we had left the Association, we found out that the non-university students had reported the incident to the police. They were able to claim with the evidence of marks and bruises on their bodies that they had been subjected to 'unprovoked' violence and beatings. The guards in the building and the people in the shops along the street could only report that we had indeed been thrashing them. They also lied to the police that we had taken over the Association and that it really should be theirs. So the police sealed the door of the Association's office with red wax.

The following day, Rashid al-Makhawi came to me and said that the cleaner at the Association had contacted him and told him that the Association's office had been sealed. Unfortunately, it was now the evening, when there was no authorised government employee whom we could contact to make a complaint.

On the third morning, I went to the Egyptian officials and explained to them that these students were not university students, and that they could not hold membership of the Association according to the rules of student associations. The officials then promptly removed the red wax from the door.

When the non-university students found out what had happened, they went back to the Egyptian officials to tell them their side of the story. The students then went and broke the lock to the headquarters of the Association and occupied it. The cleaner at the Association once again contacted Rashid al-Makhawi, and Rashid rushed over to me. He was astounded by their behaviour and I said to him, 'You are not Omani and neither am I. Why are we giving ourselves such a headache with this?!'

So we left the Association to them.

The second semester of the third year drew to a successful close. During the summer holiday, I travelled with my sister Na'ima and her husband and children to London to spend the summer there.

## *The demolition of Sharjah Fort*

Before the first semester examinations in January 1970, a friend from Sharjah contacted me by telephone to tell me that the demolition of Sharjah Fort had begun. I travelled immediately to Sharjah to stop the demolition.

There were two days left before my examinations began. I

arrived in Sharjah at night and in the morning I went to the fort. There was only one tower left in the fort, which was called the Kubs, in addition to a wall that was just a few metres high and connected to the tower.

In order to stop the demolition, I rushed to the Palace to see the Ruler of Sharjah, my brother Shaikh Khalid bin Muhammad al-Qasimi, explaining what the fort represented to the people of Sharjah.

I asked Shaikh Khalid, 'Why are you demolishing the fort?'

He replied, 'I don't want any trace of Shaikh Saqr bin Sultan al-Qasimi [the previous Ruler of Sharjah] left standing.'

I said, 'The fort is a remnant of the days of your ancestors and mine. The last vestige of Shaikh Saqr bin Sultan al-Qasimi is the Palace in which you live now, not the fort.'

Shaikh Khalid went silent. Then he said, 'Go and halt the demolition.'

'I stopped it this morning,' I told him.

I returned to the site of the fort, and took the details of the measurements of the buildings which had made up the fort. Taking the measurements was easy as the foundations were visible. I gathered up the doors and some of the wooden windows, and painted them with insect repellent. I kept them in a safe place, hoping to reinstall them in the fort at some time in the future. (In January 1996 a project to rebuild the fort was started, putting the original doors and windows back in the right places. The project was completed in April 1997 and the fort with its original doors and windows is still standing today.)

I had only one day left before the examination. On that day,

I went to Dubai airport and flew from there to Beirut, where I would take a connecting flight to Cairo. However, when I arrived in Beirut, an official at the airline company told me that there was no seat reserved for me on the flight to Cairo. I tried all the airline companies to find a seat on any flight, even if I had to travel to Europe and from there back to Cairo. But all this was to no avail.

It was one o'clock in the morning on the day of the examination when Sudan Airways announced its flight to Cairo and from there to Khartoum. Although I had visited that office before to see if I could find a seat, to no avail, I thought to myself that I should try another approach. I had always hesitated about doing it this way, but now circumstances required it. As a poet once said:

*If you find nothing other than the head of the spear to travel on,*
*Then you have no other choice but to travel on it.*

So I put a one hundred dollar note in my passport, in which my name was preceded by the title 'Shaikh'. I presented my ticket, which didn't have a reservation for Cairo, to the agent responsible for reservations at Sudan Airways, together with my passport containing the one hundred dollar note. I said, 'I have to get to Cairo this morning by any possible means.' The employee opened my passport and said, 'Welcome, our esteemed Shaikh!' as he saw the picture of Franklin D. Roosevelt on the note.

Then he rubbed out one of the names on the passenger list, and told me to go straight to the boarding area for the aircraft.

On the plane, a Sudanese passenger was sitting next to me.

Exhausted, and thinking of my looming exam, I decided to use the flight to sleep. I asked the Sudanese next to me not to wake me up, and told him that I didn't want anything to eat or drink.

After a few moments, he woke me up.

'What do you want?' I asked him.

'The hostess is asking if you want a cup of tea.'

'I told you that I don't want any tea. Now let me sleep,' I replied testily. Then I dozed off.

A few moments later, he woke me again.

I groaned, 'What do you want this time?'

'The hostess wants to know if you want breakfast.'

'I don't want anything!' I exclaimed.

I went back to sleep, but then he woke me again.

I cried, 'You must stop this. You must stop!'

He replied, '*You* must stop this, not me. I can't tolerate your snoring, which has been bothering me from the moment I got on the plane!'

At this point, the voice of the captain announced, 'Fasten your seat belts. We will reach Cairo airport in fifteen minutes.'

I got out at Cairo airport as the sun was appearing on the horizon. I rushed to complete all the entry procedures and found a taxi to take me to my house. I took my student card and my pen, and set off to the exam. I was so nervous and exhausted that I didn't pass. This was the price I paid for saving Sharjah Fort.

I completed the first semester of the fourth year, and I passed the remaining courses.

## Israeli spies

In the second semester of the fourth year of my studies, I took a course called 'Gardens and Ornamental Plants' with Dr 'Abdul-'Alim Shushan.

One day we were in the Department of Gardens and Ornamental Plants taking pictures of one another. The flower gardens were so beautiful that I felt compelled to bring a camera that took colour pictures, which I borrowed from my friend 'Ali al-'Uwais. On the afternoon of the following day 'Ubaid Yusuf al-Qasir was with me and we took pictures of the flowers and the trees, and ourselves as well. Then a guard wearing a khaki overcoat warned us, 'Photography is not allowed here!'

I exclaimed, 'There is nothing here to prohibit us taking photographs! Yesterday we were here photographing this garden.'

The guard asked, 'You! Where are you from?'

I replied, 'From the college.'

The guard asked, 'Do you have an identity card?'

'Yes,' I said.

I looked for my card, but I couldn't find it. I said, 'I left it at home.'

The guard said, 'Go in ahead of me to the college security.'

I said, 'I'm a student and I'm known in the college.'

At that very moment, one of the lecturers from the Food Industries department passed by us. I said, 'Just ask this man.' I turned to Dr Muhammad and asked, 'Dr Muhammad, do you know me?'

Dr Muhammad replied, 'Yes, I know you.'

The guard said, 'He was photographing military installations.'

Dr Muhammad fled, saying, 'I don't know this person! I've never seen him before!'

I shouted after Dr Muhammad, 'You coward!'

The guard took us to the office of the security officer on duty at the gate of the Faculty of Agriculture. There, we found a corporal who was referred to as Ambashi. He telephoned the officer on duty at his home, and said to him, 'We have seized some Israeli spies taking pictures of military installations!'

I interrupted to stop him, or in the hope that he would give me a chance to talk to Officer Salim, as I knew him very well, but to no avail. The orders given by Officer Salim to the corporal were to seize the camera and put us under guard, and then to send us to Al-Duqi Police Station.

After he had wax-sealed the camera, he couldn't find a car to take us to the police station so I suggested that the corporal put a policeman with me in my car and we could go together to the police station. I sat in the driver's seat with 'Ubaid al-Qasir at my side. The policeman sat in the back seat with the barrel of his machine gun at my neck, until we arrived at the intersection beside Orman Gardens. There were three possible roads to take:

- The right-hand road, taking us to the Giza Security Directorate
- The left-hand road, which was Al-Duqi Street, taking us to the police station
- The middle road, Al-Masaha Street, which led to my house

I took Al-Masaha Street. The policeman shouted and pushed the barrel of his machine gun further into my neck, 'Go back! Go left! Take Al-Duqi Street!'

I said, 'I will go to my house to fetch my passport, and then we will go to Al-Duqi Police Station.'

As we went down Al-Masaha Street, 'Ubaid al-Qasir said, 'Israeli spies!! If spies want to take photographs of anything, would they be carrying their cameras around and taking pictures in front of everyone?! Amazing! By God, you are idiots!'

The policeman said to 'Ubaid, 'Be quiet or I'll smack you in the face.'

I stopped the car in front of the building where I lived, and said to the policeman, 'I will get my passport and come back to you.'

He turned the barrel of his machine gun to the neck of 'Ubaid al-Qasir!

I took a long time searching for my passport. 'Ubaid al-Qasir later told me that the policeman said, 'Your friend is taking a very long time!'

'Ubaid al-Qasir had replied, 'I'll go and get him.'

'No you won't!' the policeman had said. 'I want to hand over at least one of you.'

I eventually found my passport and college identity card and we arrived at the headquarters of Internal Security. There they led us to the basement where they kept us for an hour. Then another policeman took us to the second floor, where a major called Jamal Salim asked us to take the film out of the camera. 'Ubaid al-Qasir handed over the film after taking it out of the camera. I handed over my passport and identity card. Then the major took them to another office connected to his office, and left us waiting in the second floor office.

After a brief moment, Major Jamal Salim returned. He gave me back my passport and my student card, and handed back the film to 'Ubaid al-Qasir. Then he asked us to meet his boss, whose name I can't remember. He received us in a very friendly manner, and apologised for the conduct of the guard at the college.

Once I arrived at my house that night, the telephone rang insistently. On the line was Major Shaukat Husni, from the Department of Security, who said, 'Thank God that you are alright!'

I asked, 'How did you know what happened to us?'

He replied, 'They were asking me about you.'

The next morning, everyone in the college was talking about the Israeli spies. After I had parked my car in front of the door of the college, 'Amm Ibrahim, the doorman, rushed to open the door of my car for me, and he said, 'Mr Sultan, did you know that they arrested two Israeli spies at the college yesterday?'

I set the record straight. 'Did you know that the people they arrested yesterday were me and my colleague? We were taking photographs of the gardens and the ornamental plants.'

Then the officer on duty told me about the spies, and the male and female students told me about them as well. I disabused each of them one by one, forcing me in the end to take the microphone at the main lecture theatre, which can hold more than one thousand students, before the lecture. I explained to them all what had happened. After the lecture ended, we exited out to the main road that divides the two college sections. At that point a column of tanks passed in front of us. The male and female students shouted, 'Look Sultan, look, look!' Rows of these tanks were hidden under the orange trees in the gardens.

## A plot to assassinate my brother

I completed the fourth year of my studies, and I had to repeat the year with three subjects. I spent the summer in Cairo. It came to my attention that a plan was being hatched in which a time bomb would be placed under the chair of Shaikh Khalid bin Muhammad al-Qasimi, Ruler of Sharjah, my brother, so I sought advice from Shaikh Muhammad bin Sultan al-Qasimi, who was spending the summer with his family in Cairo. He advised me to write to my brother immediately, warning him about what was going to happen,

I wrote the letter and gave it to one of my friends, who was travelling to Sharjah. I asked him to deliver it personally to Shaikh Khalid.

I telephoned my friend later in the day and he said that he had delivered the letter into the hands of Shaikh Khalid that day, 11 July 1970.

On Friday morning, 17 July 1970, Shaikh Khalid went, as he usually did, to the *majlis* at ten o'clock. The bomb had been placed under the couch that he always sat on. Through divine intervention, the time bomb had exploded at exactly nine o'clock that morning, before the Shaikh had arrived at the *majlis*. The couch and the chairs nearby had been blown into little pieces and scattered all over the place. The glass in the windows and doors of the *majlis* was shattered, but nobody was hurt.

In September 1970 I started studying to complete the required courses for the fourth year. My studies ended at the beginning of June 1971 and I spent the summer in Cairo and Alexandria. With me were my mother and my sister Na'ima with her children. In mid-August 1971, I returned to my country.

14

*The Homeland*

I RETURNED TO SHARJAH IN MID-AUGUST 1971, after completing my studies at the Faculty of Agriculture at Cairo University. One day, I parked my car near a greengrocer's shop in 'Uruba Street, and a taxi driver from Abu Dhabi stopped and asked me the way to Sharjah airport. There was a foreigner sitting in the car and he looked exhausted from travelling on the long, rough road.

I rushed from the shop with a bottle and gave it to him to drink. The man got out of the car and introduced himself. He was Carl Hegges, from the College of Agriculture, Department of Dry Land Plants, at the University of Arizona, USA. His college had a project in the Sa'diyat area of Abu Dhabi, in refrigerated greenhouse agriculture.

I introduced myself, saying, 'I am Sultan bin Muhammad al-Qasimi, agricultural engineer and graduate from the Faculty of Agriculture at Cairo University. I graduated recently. Can I give you a lift to the airport?'

Carl Hegges was hesitant about going with me to the airport, but the owner of the shop said to him, 'He is the brother of the Ruler, so don't worry.'

Carl Hegges went with me in the car. I took him to the airport to board the plane for Muscat, which had not yet landed. We sat in the airport lounge and talked about the agricultural project in Sa'diyat. After that, he made me an offer to study for a Master's degree at the College of Agriculture, in the Department of Dry Land Plants at the University of Arizona. I accepted the offer, and we agreed to correspond with each other to arrange my enrolment at the University of Arizona. However, events in Sharjah in the following months led me down a completely different path. My friendship with Carl Hegges continues to this day, however.

## Important roles and responsibilities in the government

At the beginning of October 1971, Shaikh Muhammad bin Sultan al-Qasimi asked to speak to me about his recent call on Shaikh Khalid bin Muhammad al-Qasimi, the Ruler of Sharjah. My brother, Shaikh Khalid, had told him that he would be appointing Mukhtar al-Tum, the Chairman of Sharjah Municipality, to manage his Office. Shaikh Muhammad bin Sultan al-Qasimi opposed this, saying, 'Sultan bin Muhammad al-Qasimi has come back from Cairo, and hasn't been appointed to any position in the government. He is the best person to be the Director of the Office of the Ruler.'

Shaikh Muhammad reported that my brother replied: 'You must convince Sultan to accept the position.'

Shaikh Muhammad bin Sultan al-Qasimi turned to me and said, 'Please accept this position, as it is very sensitive and you are good at dealing directly with the people.'

I accepted the position.

The office of His Highness, the Ruler of Sharjah, was a villa on Kuwait Street, in the Faiha neighbourhood of Sharjah. It was far from the *majlis* of Shaikh Khalid, where groups of people and individuals had been coming to discuss two important issues: the establishment of the United Arab Emirates and the issue of Abu Musa Island. I didn't know anything of what had gone on in the discussions about these two subjects, as I had been in Cairo all that time. So I felt that I had to learn quickly and deeply about both issues.

Concerning the first issue, the establishment of the United Arab Emirates, the opportunity for establishing a federation of six emirates, formerly the Trucial States (with the exception of Ras al-Khaimah, which was reluctant to enter the Union), had arisen after Bahrain and Qatar had gained their independence. They had previously figured in the plan for a union of nine emirates. Although Ras al-Khaimah initially had some preconditions for joining the Union the issues were resolved and it eventually joined.

An agreement had been signed between Shaikh Zayed bin Sultan Al Nahyan, Ruler of Abu Dhabi, and Shaikh Rashid bin Sa'id al-Maktoum, Ruler of Dubai. This hastened the establishment of the union of the six emirates.

On Sunday 18 July 1971 a meeting was held between the Rulers of the emirates. It was attended by Shaikh Zayed bin Sultan Al Nahyan, Ruler of Abu Dhabi; Shaikh Rashid bin Sa'id al-Maktoum, Ruler of Dubai; Shaikh Khalid bin Muhammad al-Qasimi, Ruler of Sharjah; Shaikh Muhammad bin Hamad al-Sharqi, Ruler of Fujairah; Shaikh Humaid bin Rashid al-Nu'aimi, Crown Prince of 'Ajman; and Shaikh Rashid bin Ahmad al-Mu'alla, Crown Prince of Umm al-Qaiwain. The Interim Constitution of the United Arab Emirates was signed.

The other issue was of Abu Musa Island, part of the territory of Sharjah, that was claimed by Iran. The discussion on the issue of Abu Musa Island was accelerated to find a solution between Shaikh Khalid bin Muhammad al-Qasimi, Ruler of Sharjah, and the Shah of Iran. Sir William Luce was the British Special Envoy charged with dealing with the future of Abu Musa Island. The urgency derived from the fact that Britain was committed to withdrawing its armed forces from the Gulf by the end of the year. He completed the preparations for the statement which would set the status for Abu Musa Island from May 1971 but Iran's negative attitude disrupted these talks.

On 18 August 1971, Shaikh Khalid bin Muhammad al-Qasimi sent messages to the heads of all the Arab states, explaining the findings of Britain and Iran regarding the issue of Abu Musa Island.

Shaikh Khalid bin Muhammad al-Qasimi received one response to the letters, from President Ja'far Numeiri, President of the Republic of Sudan, who gave his blessing to the deal. Shaikh Khalid also received a message from King Faisal bin 'Abdul-'Aziz Al Su'ud, King of Saudi Arabia, which stressed that the problem with Iran should be solved peacefully. King Hussein of the Hashemite Kingdom of Jordan replied that Jordan would make every possible effort to improve Arab–Iranian relations. 'Abdul Khaliq Hassuna, Secretary-General of the League of Arab States, replied that the Arab governments should communicate with the Iranian government.

Shaikh Khalid bin Muhammad al-Qasimi assigned me the task of taking a copy of the letter from King Faisal to Shaikh Zayed bin Sultan Al Nahyan, Ruler of Abu Dhabi. I travelled to Abu Dhabi on Thursday 15 October 1971 to meet Mr Ahmad bin Khalifa al-Suwaidi in his office in the Al-Manhal Palace. Attending the meeting was Mr Hamuda bin 'Ali, who was one of the officials responsible for security in Abu Dhabi at that time. The meeting with Shaikh Zayed bin Sultan Al Nahyan was arranged for the following morning. Arrangements were also made for me to spend the night at the guest house till the time of meeting.

A ceremony took place that night with a performance by the great Egyptian singer Umm Kalthoum. It was in celebration of the anniversary of the day Shaikh Zayed bin Sultan Al Nahyan became Ruler of Abu Dhabi. Mr Ahmad al-Suwaidi asked me to attend, which I did.

The following day, Ahmad al-Suwaidi came by and accompanied me to meet Shaikh Zayed bin Sultan Al Nahyan in the early morning. We met him at the *majlis* of his mother's house, as he was visiting her at that time. I met Shaikh Zayed for the first time, and gave him a copy of the letter from King Faisal. After he had read the letter, we had a talk in the presence of Mr Ahmad al-Suwaidi. It became apparent that he wasn't happy about the arrangements concerning Abu Musa Island.

Several days later, I was assigned the task of taking the copy of the letter from King Faisal to the Government of Egypt. In Egypt, I met Mr Mahmoud Riyad, Foreign Minister of Egypt, and gave him a copy of the letter.

At the end of October 1971, I returned from Cairo. On 1 November 1971, a number of items were published in the newspaper *Al-Khaleej* which had been founded by two brothers, Taryam bin 'Umran and 'Abdullah bin 'Umran. The newspaper was licensed in Sharjah and printed in Kuwait. It published excerpts from the secret discussions between Shaikh Khalid bin Muhammad al-Qasimi, Ruler of Sharjah, and Sir William Luce, British Special Envoy, dealing with the future of Abu Musa Island. Statements by Shaikh Khalid bin Muhammad al-Qasimi made headlines on the front page of that newspaper. The few words of the headlines gave the impression that Shaikh Khalid had firmly rejected the suggestion put forward by Sir William Luce regarding the future of the island. The printed details of the discussions, however, had indicated that Shaikh Khalid felt that the suggestion could be the last resort to preserve our rights and sovereignty over the island under the prevailing circumstances.

The Ministry of Information in Kuwait was asked to order the confiscation of the 1 November issue, which had already been printed. The number of copies was an estimated four thousand, all of which were destroyed. However, the news agencies conveyed the information that had been published in the *Al-Khaleej* newspaper, and published it again in the second edition on the morning of 2 November. Sir William Luce was distressed by the news when it reached him that evening, so he contacted Shaikh Khalid bin Muhammad al-Qasimi and urged him to immediately revoke the licence of the *Al-Khaleej* newspaper. Shaikh Khalid replied that such a decision would create internal security problems, and he promised that the newspaper would not publish any more articles about Abu Musa Island. That evening, 'Abdullah bin 'Umran, the Editor-in-Chief, promised Shaikh Khalid bin Muhammad al-Qasimi that no article would be published about Abu Musa. However, pressure to revoke the licence of the *Al-Khaleej* newspaper continued, ending only when 'Abdullah bin 'Umran wrote a letter to Shaikh Khalid bin Muhammad al-Qasimi on 10 November 1971, promising that nothing would be published about the ongoing talks concerning the Arab islands in the Gulf.

## *The Abu Musa agreement with Iran*

At precisely seven o'clock on 30 November 1971, Shaikh Khalid bin Muhammad al-Qasimi, Ruler of Sharjah, declared in a long speech that an agreement had been concluded between the Iranian government and himself. This agreement consisted of the following points:

- The agreement does not affect Sharjah's view of its sovereignty over Abu Musa Island.
- Abu Musa Island will be divided between a part for Sharjah and the other part for Iran.
- The flag of Sharjah shall continue to be raised on the flagpole of the Sharjah Police on the Island.
- The Sharjah Police and the Island's administration shall continue to operate in the remaining (Sharjah) part after the division of the Island.
- The citizens there shall be under the sovereignty of Sharjah.

On the morning of 1 December 1971, a delegation headed by Shaikh Saqr bin Muhammad al-Qasimi, the Deputy Ruler, went from Sharjah to meet the Iranian delegation which had come to the island. That evening, demonstrations broke out, not only in Sharjah, but in most of the emirates, in rejection of the arrangements. The protestors did not want to give away any part of the island to Iran, now or ever.

The delegation headed by Shaikh Saqr bin Muhammad al-Qasimi returned after sunset that day. When Shaikh Saqr was about enter his house that night, a shot was fired at him, penetrating his body but without causing serious injury. The identity of the gunman was never discovered.

## *Birth of the State*

The state of the United Arab Emirates was born on the morning of 2 December 1971. The Rulers of six emirates (with the exception of Ras al-Khaimah) gathered in the guest house in Jumaira (Dubai). This was after each Ruler had signed the agreement in their respective emirate to end the special agreements between them and the British on 1 December 1971. As the Rulers gathered, this was the first meeting of the Supreme Council of the State of the United Arab Emirates, activating the Interim Constitution. Shaikh Zayed bin Sultan Al Nahyan was elected President of the State of the United Arab Emirates; Shaikh Rashid bin Sa'id al-Maktoum was elected Deputy President of the State of the United Arab Emirates; and Shaikh Maktoum bin Rashid al-Maktoum was elected Prime Minister.

At that meeting, discussions on the relationship between the fledgling nation and the British government were held. The discussion concluded with the signing of a friendship agreement between the State of the United Arab Emirates and the British government. Members of the Supreme Council of the Union authorised Shaikh Zayed bin Sultan Al Nahyan, as President of the State, to sign the agreement alongside the British Political Resident in Bahrain, who was there on behalf of the British government.

On 9 December, the Council of Ministers was formed under the chairmanship of Shaikh Maktoum bin Rashid al-Maktoum. I was asked to serve as the Minister of Education and I accepted. I also maintained my position as Director General of the Office of the Ruler of Sharjah.

## Days of hardship: the assassination of my brother the Ruler of Sharjah

On the morning of Monday 8 Dhul-Hijjah 1391 AH, corresponding to 24 January 1972, I was in my office at the Office of His Highness, the Ruler, when Khalid al-'Alami, Director of Sharjah Finance Department, came in carrying his briefcase to tell me that Shaikh Khalid would be coming to the office to sign some bank cheques for the government salaries and contracts. This was owing to the fact that the Eid holiday fell on 26 January that year. A short time later, some people from the special guard of Shaikh Khalid came and told me that he was on his way, and that they had come to make sure the place was safe.

At eleven o'clock that morning, Shaikh Khalid arrived. He asked Khalid al-'Alami to present to him the matters which required signatures, and asked me to sit by his side. When he had signed all the cheques, he turned to Khalid al-'Alami and said, 'From the beginning of next month, Sultan will sign all the cheques.'

Khalid al-'Alami said, 'That is a heavy responsibility.'

Shaikh Khalid remarked, 'When Sultan is in my place, I will be more relaxed. I want to rest.'

Khalid al-'Alami said, 'Your Highness, you could travel somewhere to relax.'

Shaikh Khalid responded, 'I need a long rest.'

As we were leaving the office of His Highness, the Ruler, at noon, Shaikh Khalid asked me to go with him to have lunch in the Palace. His wife was not in the Palace, as she had been invited to a wedding feast.

In the Palace, Shaikh Khalid asked me to wait for him in the sitting room, as he wanted to take a bath. I said, 'I want to go to the house to fetch some documents to show you.'

It was close to two o'clock in the afternoon. I lived in the same house as Shaikh Su'ud bin Sultan al-Qasimi, my sister's husband, and it was not far from the Palace. When I left the house to go to the Palace, I met Mr Rashid bin 'Ali bin Dimas, a prominent construction contractor, who asked me to sign a bank cheque which Khalid al-'Alami had not given to Shaikh Khalid to sign.

Rashid bin Dimas said, 'Khalid al-'Alami told me that all the cheques would be signed by Sultan.'

I said, 'But from the first of the month.'

Rashid bin Dimas said, 'Al-'Alami said that he would make the arrangements with the bank.'

'I am going to the Palace,' I said. 'Shaikh Khalid will sign it, and in the afternoon I will send you the cheque.'

It was half past two when we heard gunshots fired at the Palace. Rashid bin Dimas asked me about it, and I told him that some guards were holding exercises behind the Palace. Then we heard the sound of a bomb exploding, and smoke came from the entrance to the Palace, where the Shaikh lived. The Palace was on a hill and one could see who entered or left through the door of the Palace from the house of Shaikh Su'ud bin Sultan al-Qasimi, which was also on a hill.

I asked Rashid bin Dimas to ride with me as I went to the side gate of the Palace, which was made for the family and employees to enter, and through which the attackers had entered the Palace. When I got close to the gate, shots from a machine gun struck my car from whoever was there. We lowered our heads and changed direction to the Faiha neighbourhood, where the British Head of the Sharjah Police, Mr Burns, lived. I told him to bring soldiers of the Union Defence Force, and I returned to the house of my sister Na'ima bint Muhammad al-Qasimi. She had been talking with her brother, Shaikh Khalid, when the attack began. He said to her, 'Saqr bin Sultan is inside the Palace.'

I contacted my brother, Shaikh Saqr bin Muhammad al-Qasimi. My sister had told him about what happened, and I asked him, 'Are you in charge?' He said, 'No, you are in charge. I am busy with the shooting. I'm besieging the Palace from the southern side, and the guards who are there in the facilities of the general *majlis* will have besieged the Palace from the northern side. I do not want any of the assailants to escape.'

My brother, Shaikh Saqr bin Muhammad al-Qasimi, had taken up a position on the roof of his house on the hill, which overlooked the Palace of the Ruler, where two light machine guns on bipods were firing at long range.

At precisely half past three in the afternoon – an hour after the incident began – the Union Defence Forces arrived, accompanied by the Head of the Sharjah Police, at the house of Shaikh Su'ud bin Sultan al-Qasimi. I was there, and as I was telling them that the Palace had been attacked by a group of men led by Shaikh Saqr bin Sultan al-Qasimi, the previous Ruler of Sharjah, who had been exiled from Sharjah by the British several years earlier, shots rained down from the Palace. We also heard the sound of two hand grenades exploding in the Palace courtyard. Attempts to infiltrate the Palace were made by some of the special forces of the Shaikh's guard, which were sent to occupy the outer walls of the Palace, and these were met by concentrated gunfire.

The situation was very difficult, as Shaikh Khalid bin Muhammad al-Qasimi, his children and servants were in the Palace, so I asked the commander of the Union Defence Forces to avoid any action that would result in injury to Shaikh Khalid and his children.

After making sure that the children of Shaikh Khalid bin Muhammad al-Qasimi had moved to the villa in the Palace grounds at the beginning of the attack, the order was given to attack the palace with the Union Forces and members of the Sharjah Palace Guard. The side gate of the Palace was kept occupied, along with all the Palace walls, by a hail of gunfire and thick smoke for cover.

The siege of the Palace and the inner grounds was complete. There were no movements in the Palace as the firing continued on the windows. The bullets went into the corridors, halls and other rooms inside the Palace.

At half past four the following morning, Shaikh Muhammad bin Rashid al-Maktoum, Defence Minister of the United Arab Emirates, arrived at the house of Su'ud bin Sultan al-Qasimi. He was accompanied by a Saudi representative, 'Abdullah al-Fadhl, who had come with an offer from King Faisal 'Abdul-'Aziz Al Su'ud, the King of Saudi Arabia, to Shaikh Saqr bin Sultan al-Qasimi. The offer was that he would be taken to Saudi Arabia if he handed over Shaikh Khalid bin Muhammad al-Qasimi unscathed.

Shaikh Muhammad bin Rashid al-Maktoum asked me to take him to a telephone so that he could talk to Shaikh Saqr bin Sultan al-Qasimi along with 'Abdullah al-Fadhl.

Shaikh Muhammad bin Rashid al-Maktoum talked with Shaikh Saqr bin Sultan al-Qasimi by telephone, and put the Saudi offer to him. However, Shaikh Saqr bin Sultan al-Qasimi replied, 'Shaikh Khalid bin Muhammad al-Qasimi has been killed.'

Shaikh Muhammad bin Rashid al-Maktoum said, 'Then surrender.'

At six o'clock that morning, Shaikh Saqr bin Sultan al-Qasimi surrendered along with his companions, and they were put in prison.

## Selection of the new Ruler

That morning, 25 January, a family meeting was arranged for eleven o'clock in the house of Shaikh Hamad bin Majid al-Qasimi and I was determined to participate in it.

In front of the gate to the house of Shaikh Su'ud I found a group of guards of the deceased Shaikh Khalid, his car, the driver and his military guard. They ushered me into the car and we went to the *majlis* of Shaikh Hamad bin Majid al-Qasimi. Members of the Qasimi family had filled the whole place, except for one space on the main couch in the centre of the *majlis*. Shaikh Khalid bin Khalid al-Qasimi, the most senior member of the family, was sitting on the left side, so I took my place on the main couch in the centre of the *majlis*.

Shaikh Khalid bin Khalid al-Qasimi was sitting down as he talked about matters relevant to the family. After that, Shaikh Muhammad bin Sultan al-Qasimi stood up. He had been sitting in the middle of the row at the left side of the *majlis*. He said, 'There are more important matters than this. Your ship is in danger. It needs someone to steer it to safety. It doesn't matter whether he is our eldest or youngest, but he has to be someone who can shoulder this responsibility. That person is Sultan bin Muhammad al-Qasimi.'

The *majlis* was filled with the sound of unanimous approval.

I remained silent for some time. Shaikh Muhammad bin Sultan al-Qasimi came over to me and held out his hand. I shook his hand and sat with him on the couch.

Members of the family swarmed around me, kissing me and giving me their blessings. Shaikh Muhammad bin Sultan al-Qasimi held my hand, and didn't let go until he kissed me.

Then I said: 'Help me to be a faithful son to my elders, a sincere brother to my contemporaries, and a kind father to the young.'

Early in the morning of Wednesday 10 Dhul-Hijjah, the day of Eid al-Adha in the year 1391 AH, corresponding to 26 January 1972, people rushed to the Eid prayer area. The Eid prayers were held and we listened to an account of the good things that the deceased Shaikh had done in his life and we said prayers for forgiveness for him.

After that, the funeral prayer was held and the body was taken to the Jubail Cemetery in Sharjah, where we buried him. May God have mercy on him. He lived among us in piety and uprightness.

In the general *majlis* I received the well-wishers who had come both to show their support for me and to give their condolences for the deceased:

– May God grant you great consolation . . .

– We congratulate you on Eid . . .

– May God wash away your sadness . . .

– We congratulate you on your appointment as Ruler.

# Index of People

291

# A NOTE ON THE AUTHOR

Born in 1939, Shaikh Sultan bin Muhammad al-Qasimi is the author of several books including *The Myth of Arab Piracy in the Gulf* (1986), *The British Occupation of Aden* (1990) and *The Fragmentation of the Omani Empire* (1989).

# A NOTE ON THE TYPE

The text of this book is set Adobe Garamond. It is one of several versions of Garamond based on the designs of Claude Garamond. It is thought that Garamond based his font on Bembo, cut in 1495 by Francesco Griffo in collaboration with the Italian printer Aldus Manutius. Garamond types were first used in books printed in Paris around 1532. Many of the present-day versions of this type are based on the *Typi Academiae* of Jean Jannon cut in Sedan in 1615.

Claude Garamond was born in Paris in 1480. He learned how to cut type from his father and by the age of fifteen he was able to fashion steel punches the size of a pica with great precision. At the age of sixty he was commissioned by King Francis I to design a Greek alphabet, for this he was given the honourable title of royal type founder. He died in 1561.